The Greenwood Wo

For everyone who wants to set it up

The English Translation of this Book

This translation was kindly taken over by Carola Schulz, the English teacher of our school and a very close friend. She put a lot of effort into it. Thank you so much, Carola, without you this English version of my book wouldn't exist.

But there are really obvious shortcomings of this translation. Though, I let the book proofread by quite a few native English speaking friends, the work to make it a well written English book is simply too big and time consuming for me.

A big thank you to all the ladies and gentlemen who gave me a helping hand in proofreading! I appreciate all your input but I finally decided to shoot the text out as it is with all its problems and without many changes.

I'm sure, dear reader, you will understand all the facts despite they are in English written by two Germans. I'm so sorry for this. I just don't have the time for corrections anymore aside my regular work as a teacher.

That is the reason why I give a discount for this English version of the book.

I hope for a knowing smile on your face if you stumble over strange text and uncommon sentences.

Have a good read though!

Michael Stibane

Preface

For sure there has been a reason to write this book. Getting familiar with greenwood craft and setting up a neat workshop with all essential tools and appliances took me roughly three years. Mike Abbott's first greenwood book from the 90s in its umpteenth edition, the forum bodgers.org.uk and various attempts to search the web led to the knowledge I have gained. So step by step I have learned more about this topic, mostly in English. Three years? That is pretty much time for someone who loves to be productive and wants to create things with his very own hands. But in German such a book, which deals with the setting up of a greenwood workshop, doesn't exist. For that reason I would like to share my knowledge on these pages – typical for a teacher, isn't it. By the way my main occupation is teacher in adult education.

During my search for tools, instructions, pictures, reports on experience and videos I found scanned pages of a small British booklet of the Young Farmers Association from the 1950s with the title "Tools and devices for coppice crafting" and was written by F. Lambert. Coppicing is called "Niederwaldwirtschaft" in German. The author explained in the brochure tools, appliances, devices and machines which are needed by a young farmer to get an extra income by crafting wood products from small diameter wood.

Because my first occupation was cutting machine operator which meant I served an apprenticeship in toolmaking and also my inoculated woodworking virus by my great-grandfather Willy let my fingers itch to setting up things by trial and error without any measurements.

Trial and error is that what I intend to spare you from by giving measurements because trial and error cost time and money.

I have been earning my living or better surviving money with writing since 2003. In the beginning I was working as a freelancer and later as a journalist and editor for computer magazines, mainly in the section Linux and Open-Source. My colleagues had already written books about IT-related topics. After compiling a successful article, the Hanser-Verlag, a publishing agency, called me and offered me to write a book about databases. I rejected because it is time-consuming and three to six months' work would not be in the relation to the earnings. Still, it seemed that I had the guts, otherwise such an established publisher would not have asked me. That moment I decided to write a book one day in my life. Now it is done. But I took me a little more than one year to finish it.

It is typical to publish illustrated step-by-step instructions for longer or difficult tasks in computer magazines. This kind of instructions became a second nature for me. And so I published some photo series about green woodworking on my Facebook profile and shared them among various greenwood groups in social networks. The reactions on them were very positive and the explanations were helpful for a lot of people. The results and reactions motivated me to make more out of it and to publish them in a book.

Now it is done, this book about setting up a greenwood workshop. Because I publish the book myself, it might have some weaknesses in its structure, its quality of photos or even in its style. Referring to grammar or spelling I am hoping I was aware of all small and big mistakes and corrected them adequately. But I cannot be 100% sure.

I would ask you to overlook my sins which I might have conducted on my first attempt.

At Academy-Award-Ceremonies and other events of that kind it is common to say thank you to all and everyone. My cat's name is Oskar. So then my special thanks to Oskar because he took care of my patient wife while I was away either on markets, presentations of my wood-working or even in my workshop and on my computer writing this book at home.

Obviously you are interested in the topic „greenwood", otherwise you wouldn't hold this book in your hands. Therefore I stop swaggering now and let you read ... and try ... and make ... and ...

Have fun!

Your Michael Stibane (Stibs) and certainly Oskar

Contents

Truly hand-made:
Greenwood Craft

Working with Hand Tools

Do you know the problem with having a Sunday's rest? As soon as you turn your radio louder because they are playing your favourite music on a Sunday or even a holiday, so that you can listen to it all around your house, some neighbours might call the police for disturbance of the peace. And woe betide you, you dare to use the lawn mower or a garden pump while some signs insisting on noise reduction! Immediate damnation to hell simply results in that. By far worse could be the result if you suddenly start your machinery to enjoy your favourite hobby. But working with hand tools cannot be surpassed by its peace. The one or other hit with your hammer is short enough that neighbours accept it. Out of my own experience I can grant you, that it is fun to see a blackbird not even two metres away waiting if the wood shavings really aren't edible worms while interrupting work for a moment.

Besides the obvious peace the use of hand tools provides further advantages while working. It doesn't matter if you are an adult or a child. It is enormously satisfying to hold the result of your work in your very own hands. As a six-year old I was damn proud of building my sand castle surrounded by a water ditch on the beach of the Baltic Sea.

As a twelve-year old I made my first water wheel from the remaining wood parts of my great-grandfather within an hour and watched it for ages. When I was nineteen my journeyman's piece as a mechanic got built into a milling machine and was really used for production, that moment I grinned like a Cheshire cat. With thirty my favourite toy was my out of single parts self-assembled computer. And today, with 45 years, I build water wheels for my seven-year-old neighbour's daughter Laura in absence of own grandchildren (still). For sure you might know that wonderful feeling out of your own experience. I promise you, it will return swiftly, if you accomplish your work with hand tools.

A further advantage becomes visible in your electricity bill. A small drilling machine needs six hundred Watt, a lathe already eight hundred and a router, pride of a craftsman, who works with it, the same. If these machines only run eight hours in seven days makes it five Euros per week, 20 Euros per month and 240 Euros per year, having a fixed price of 0.30 Euro per Kilowatt hour.

That is already half of the price of setting up a workshop like you will see in this book. Working by hand might not be fast, accurate in tenth of millimetres and efficient – especially in the beginning – but it is unbeatable in reference to environmental friendliness and your wallet. One day a Sunday walker had a look at my workshop when I was woodturning a small candleholder on my pole lathe and said: „You have already made your energy transition". With that I agree.

Advantages of manual work

If you work with your very own hands and do not use any engine-driven tools, you do not disturb any person or animal in its peace. The creation of objects and values with your very own hands is an immensely satisfying activity. Normally you know the origin and the history of an item. Can you say this about a bowl you bought at a supermarket?
The work with hand tools spares your wallet and the environment. You do not need any electricity.

Advantages and Disadvantages of Greenwood

This book is about setting up a workshop for working with green, which means fresh-cut wood. At DIY-stores you can usually buy only dried wood. The same applies to joineries. These put a lot of effort in adequate storing the wood for production to keep it dry. And now wet greenwood? Indeed! The doubtlessly biggest advantage of greenwood is its easy processing. Because we work with hand tools, the physical effort is by far lower than by processing the material in its dried condition.

A second issue is its availability. Dried wood for joineries has a maximum moisture content. This wood can only be purchased at a wood trader. Are you in the woods and find a broken-down branch at the weekend, then you cannot process it straight away the next day. Depending on its diameter, the kind of wood or currently occurring rainy weather you need to think about a longer drying period up to several months as well as the appropriate drying process.

In the case of greenwood you take a log of a currently felled old fruit tree, split it, cut it to the right length and start straight away. Besides the period for drying even the used energy plays a certain role. Wood from the DIY-store got mostly kiln dried. The producer wastes lots of energy to detract water out of the wood in huge heated plants. Hopefully this procedure has its right to be for industrial production (in case environmental legislation did all correctly) but in my opinion it is not always necessary for wood used for craft and hobby. With the use of greenwood you simply work environmentally-friendly.

Of course there are also disadvantages of greenwood. As it is a natural material. You never know what to expect in a log which lies in front of you. With some experience you are able to assess with the help of outer signs if it has grown straight and without any knotholes but you still have no idea what might be hidden underneath the bark. And so there can be some bad surprises if the wood is split. A hidden knothole is exactly at the position, where you wanted to carve the bowl of a spoon. The tree has grown twisted and I really need straight fibre for chair legs. Or you have wood from a fast-grown tree with wide annual rings which are not so solid like from a slowly-grown tree. Or the worst – an absolute catastrophe – a small piece of the blade of my expensive chisel breaks off because of a grown-in nail which was driven in the tree to fix a bird house ages ago. You definitely have to be aware of such surprises while working with greenwood.

Greenwood is dried <u>after</u> its processing. While drying the wood changes its shape. For instance, if you wood-turn a perfect cylinder from sapwood it will look oval afterwards.

This is due to the fact that during the drying process the wood shrinks radial and tangential differently. A further fact is the already mentioned twisted-grown wood. Here you can only be prepared for surprises because you never know how the dried wood will look like. Sometimes you will be astonished about your small piece of artwork in interaction with your skills and Mother

Nature. The radial and tangential shrinking has also another negative effect. Fine cracks might appear in the wood. Certainly there are some techniques to avoid or diminish cracks but to be completely sure you can only be if a faultless result is there in the end.

Advantages of greenwood

The wood still contains water and is therefore softer and easier to work with. This fact is most important for the use of hand tools because you need less power to process it.
Greenwood is available everywhere and at any time. Is a tree cut, you can ask for a log or a few branches and start straight away. The drying is done after the processing.
Greenwood needs no additional energy to get dried like milled wood available at a DIY-store. You work in close relation with nature and energy-efficiently.

Disadvantages of greenwood

You have to be prepared for surprises while working with greenwood. Anomalies of growth like branches or twists are possible. Even traces of human influences, like a nail in a tree, can disturb your work significantly.
While drying your piece of work there can be irregularities. The wood shrinks radial and tangential differently. Due to that there can be tensions which probably can lead to drying cracks.

Greenwood in the Days gone by

At this point I have no intention to write about a Neanderthal man who took a branch to beat up a mammoth. Rather I would like to speak about a time which dates back roughly one hundred years.

The landscape, where the things came to pass, is the eastern region of the Ore Mountains (Erzgebirge) south of Dresden. I grew up here. The old village-mill was the last house in the village and more than one hundred metres away from the next house. Next to it was a mountain called Gittelberg ("Gittel" is an old German word for "small farmstead") with cow's pastures, fields and forests, behind it followed meadows, the village's brook and more forest.

As early as the middle ages my village had already been founded as a so called Waldhufendorf, a characteristic type of village in this region. Along a waterway settlers built their houses and cleared in wide stripes the forest (Wald) behind them to have space for their fields and pastures, the so called "Hufen" (farmsteads with land for the survival of a family of three or maximum five). The border to the neighbour was not recognisable back then. However on the mountain fields there lay a lot of stone all around. These were collected and then heaped up at the borders or piled neatly. So the landscape-shaping dry stone walls and stone ridges of the Ore Mountains were created. Bushes and trees started to grow on these rock formations.

Behind the mill of Müglitz – stone ridges border fields. (Source: Wikipedia)

About 1900 these bushes and trees were still intensively used by the farmer who owned the stone ridge. Every seven to twenty years he cut the trees down to its stump and used it as firewood, for producing tools for work on his farmstead or even for handcrafting. He sold the handcrafted products and received an additional income. The wood carvers and wood turners of the Ore Mountains became world-famous for their work. The village of Seiffen, maybe 50 kilometres away from my home village, is well known for its hoop turning technology. Try to find a video of this technique online and you'll be stunned. The tree stumps of the cut-down trees and bushes were sprouting again and so after a couple of years there was usable wood again. In forestry this kind of rotating use is known as coppicing.

After World War II this use of wood of the stone ridges came nearly to a still stand because cheap industrial products and other reasons made it unnecessary. The shaft of my garden hoe is broken. Today we solve the problem the following way: We go to the next DIY-store and buy a new shaft. At the turn of the century the farmer went behind his house. One hundred metres away stood a hazel bush. There he cut off a straight shoot in the right diameter and left the leaves and twigs there to rot. On a shaving horse he debarked the hazel shoot with a drawknife, fitted it to the hoe and fixed it with a nail – done. It all had to dry during the crafting process and the use of the hoe. But usually a farmer is a wise man and had a bundle of already dried hazel shoots stored in his shed for such cases.

Products made from greenwood were shafts and handles for tools or furnishings like shelves, racks, milking stools or chairs and garden furniture. Toys like spinning tops or a carved whistle, a water wheel, arrow and bow and a slingshot were crafted that way too. Did the farmer even own a lathe in his barn, he could wood turn smokers and nutcrackers in winter.

From birch twigs he made besoms and brooms, which he could use to clean his stable or yard and there still is no artificial substitute to it. Containers and baskets were either crafted from willow rods or from ash, spruce or oak sapwood stripes (splint).

Today these activities are summarized under the term "rural craft". Most of the time the durability of the products was higher compared to items in the fast-moving consumer society. Have we forgotten the old skills and knowledge?

The wood-turned and carved wooden toys became symbols of the settlements of the Ore Mountains, e.g. here Olbernhau. (Source: Wikipedia)

Some still remember it: The generation 40+ often watches in astonishment my workshop and is delighted to see things from their childhood. At medieval and craft markets you find the one or other pole lathe turner, spoon carver or broom-maker.

The wood carvers still run their artful craft. Even basket-makers are seen as artists and keepers of the old knowledge and they share their skills with children in environmental educational institutions and craft lessons in schools. The traditional, closed-to-nature and energy-efficient crafting still doesn't enjoy the reputation like it used to have in the old times. I am very pleased that you hold this book in your hands, so obviously you share my thoughts.

Greenwood-Crafting...

... did exist in the good old time. Today it is better known as „rural craft".

... can produce the basic necessities, furniture, toys, tools, containers or artwork. Nearly everything, what is made from „normal wood", can also be crafted out of greenwood.

... often finds too little appreciation in our throw-away society and only a few can pass on skills and knowledge of the old people to the younger generations.

Wood and Environment

After a short trip to the history of the Ore Mountains back to practical things. Test yourself what you might remember from your biology lessons. Trees are plants. They have perfected the process of photosynthesis. There the aerial carbon dioxide is transformed by the help of sun rays into carbon and is stored as wood by the assistance of nutrients and water taken via roots from the soil. Trees are natural regulators for the carbon dioxide-content in our atmosphere and fight actively the greenhouse effect. Are you asking yourself now, why do the cut down the rainforest in the Amazon region while global warming leads to melting glaciers? Economic short-termed profit aims are more appreciated and wanted than keeping and protecting our environment.

Woodland in Holzhau, Eastern Ore Mountains (Source: WP)

But let us stay in Germany. The second National Forestry Inventory (2001 – 2003) stated that 31 percent of the area of Germany is covered with forest. Nevertheless, the settled area, which means living spaces and industrial territories, grows and at the same time the forested area increases as well. That is mainly the result of reforestation. Due to that fact Germany counts to one of the most densely wooded countries within the European Union. Therefore the forest is an important part of our environment. Besides aerial carbon dioxide-reduction it has a big influence on the regional water balance and soil erosion. It is a recreational retreat for humans and also home to countless species of animals and plants and surely a valuable economic factor.

Would we burn the wood that we collect to heat our homes, there would be no additional carbon dioxide-emissions in relation what a tree has used before to grow. That means wood as the source of heat and energy is neutral in comparison to fossil fuels. But wouldn't it be much better to store wood for years or centuries to detract climate gas out of the air? So we could compensate at least a small part of environmental damages. This storage we should combine with an appropriate use of wood. And here the greenwood crafting becomes reality: The wooden hay-rake, the breakfast board made from beech or a festive smoker store aerial carbon dioxide for years or even decades. The amount might be extremely small but it is definitely better to do small things than nothing.

Forest...

... covers 31 percent of the area of Germany. The forested area grows permanently year by year. Germany is one of the most densely wooded countries in the EU.

... is tremendously important for humans, animals and plants. A forest means home, recreation and quality of life. It is important for the reduction of aerial carbon dioxide and the regulation of the water balance.

... is the basis for our greenwood workshop. Our long-lasting products detract atmospheric carbon for several years and contribute to a cleaner environment.

Thoughts for Pedagogues and Therapists

I am quite convinced that you have already known the facts that I had written in the previous section. But now a crucial test: What kind of wood is used to produce matches? My wife answered: "dried wood." And so, many people will react like her. I suppose the number of people who know that such a bare utensil is mostly made of poplar is rather small. In my opinion it is vital to know what raw material was used to recognize its value better. The value is even higher if you have seen the tree personally and you might even know stories about it. Both parents and teachers mediate values to children in school and free time.

Since 1870 the Swedish have been calling the mediation of valued at schools: Slöjd. In the English speaking world the subject is known as sloyd. In schools of the former GDR and in Bavarian schools, which are known to me, this was and is called craft lessons. Two aspects are aim of these lessons. On the one hand it is the mediation of knowledge about materials like wood or metal. And so the theoretical knowledge for instance from lessons in biology and physics can be used practically. On the other hand there is the mediation of crafting skills while working with these materials. Whatever this type of lesson is called, at the end it is important that a child knows the basics about a material and also the difficulties of its processing with tools to make a useful product out of it. The pride of a child at the end of a lesson to show the finished product to its parents and others is motivation to learn more on this subject and to get better with the use of tools. Craft lessons train various skills including a creative mind, which is able to transfer the known use of a tool and a particular material into new situations.

Since 2012 I have been teaching computer topics to prisoners in the penal institution Dresden. Our class room is directly next to the work therapy aka occupational therapy. An ergo therapist is employed to accompany the psychic or physical impaired prisoners. Most important working material is wood.

Only in Bavaria and Baden-Wuerttemberg exists the profession occupational therapist. In all other German states it is part of the apprenticeship of an ergo therapist. The occupational therapist Ewald Schadt founded and run successfully a wildwood project[1] in Niederweiler. Unfortunately it doesn't exist anymore. The institution took care of long-term unemployed people and their reintegration in society.

An important field of Schadt's work was greenwood craft which supported and developed crafting skills and provided a meaningful activity for the unemployed to make their way easier back into a „normal life". With reference to the above-mentioned examples you can see the supportive therapeutic effect of

---

[1] http://www.wildholz-projekt.de

greenwood crafting. It is a useful activity. People can define themselves about it and find back to their own identity. With the smallest effort quick success can be reached with green woodwork. With a simple knife and a piece of wood you can create something useful. These easy-to-reach goals are highly motivating.

Learning and therapy

Greenwood crafting can be excellently used in craft lessons for children, teenagers and adults. Besides it can play a vital part in teaching environmental issues because with it you are able to support the complex topic "forest" and its importance and influence on our environment.

Greenwood crafting can also be used in treating psychic and physical impairments. The influence of useful work and fast-reaching results has a positive effect.

Various Kinds of Wood

The following chapter introduces endemic deciduous tree species which I have worked with. That kind of wood you also will be using in greenwood crafting to create things out of it. In principle there exists no wood which wouldn't be suitable for something. If you can get a fallen or freshly cut tree, take it. When I started with greenwood crafting in 2011 I took any kind of wood just to have material to work with. Over time there have been opening up new sources, so the lack of wood has decreased as well.

Although I gained experience by working with spruce and pine wood, it is much better to work with deciduous tree species in greenwood crafting. Coniferous wood is long-fibred and tends to splinter. Even the content of resin is very high, so a shaft made of spruce wood might smell well but it is sticky and leads to stains on the skin, which gets hardly off by using normal soap. But still you can use spruce (shingles, splint baskets) or yew (traditionally to make arrows) to craft a lot of items.

The following listing and description of woods is limited to some important endemic deciduous trees in Germany. To find information on rather exotic trees like Common Lilac (Syringa vulgaris) or Magnolia (Magnolia x soulangiana) check the internet or even try the wood yourself. The appendix of this book contains an overview of tree species in Latin, English, French, and German because you find heaps of information on greenwood crafting at the internet in different languages and it is good to know what kind of wood is explained or described on that particular page.

The description of the kinds of wood is divided into three parts. First I mention general information on the tree, add a brief trivia and write about my own experience.

Then follow characteristics of the tree like habitat preferences or appearance characteristics. The third part deals with the wood of the tree and its use – for sure the most interesting part for you.

White Willow (Salix Alba)

There are various kinds of willows and all of them can be summarized with one generic term. For instance White Willow, Goat Willow and Basket Willow are widely spread. The different species can have very different characteristics. Anyway, representative for them I am writing here about the White Willow (Salix Alba), whose wood I have been working with.

White Willow leaves (Source: Wikipedia)

Characteristics:

White Willows prefer wet ground near the banks of brooks and on the edges of ponds. The tree grows up to 30 metres in height. The narrow and lancet-shaped leaves shimmer silvery. If branches reach to the ground, they easily form roots. Willow's bark contains Salicin which our body transforms into salicylic acid and acts antipyretic.

Wood:

White Willow is often cut as pollarded willow in winter time and over the year the annual shoots are made to baskets. Older shoots can be made to walking sticks. The actual wood, light sapwood with a darker core is used less often but it is relatively good for wood turning and carving. Since the wood is very fibrous, you need very sharp tools to get a clean cut. Sometimes it is better to leave the willow dry for a while. This process is called "mellowing" among the green woodworkers. Especially for bowl turning the mellowing is useful.

European White Birch (Betula Pendula)

Birch trees are pioneer trees because they are the first ones which grow on fallow land and reclaim it. In Scandinavia and Russia they have a status in the awareness of people like oak or linden trees have for people in Germany – kind of a national tree. Bark and leaves contain, very much like willow trees, Salicin which is transformed in the body and soothes pain and fever. In spring birch trees are spudded to win birch sap which can be processed to birch wine or hair tonic and it is assumed to be healthy. Birch wood contains a lot of terpenes and so it burns even as freshly cut wood.

Birch trees in autumn (Source: Wikipedia)

Characteristics:

Birch trees do not have any particular demands on the ground they grow. The white bark stands out in comparison to the dark forest and the hanging branches with fresh green are a symbol for spring. The leaves are four to seven centimetres long and rhombus-shaped with a long tip. Birch trees grow very fast.

Wood:

The use of birch wood in greenwood crafting is almost unlimited. From the bark you can win birch tar (bitumen-like glue and sealant, known since ancient times) or it is used to make boxes and sheaths out of it. The tight roots are used as substitutes for short strings. From the thin branches you can make brooms and besoms. A birch tree only has sapwood and this is an excellent material for wood turning and carving. Starting with tools handles to chair legs, spoons, containers and even toys can be crafted out of it. I prefer to craft kuksas (wooden cups), bowls, shrink pots and spoons from birch wood. The wood rots very fast if used in outdoor areas.

Copper or Common Beech (Fagus Sylvatica)

„Look for beech trees" („Buchen sollst Du suchen.") is a German proverb while a thunderstorm comes up. For a greenwood worker beech wood is a popular kind of wood. The tree has pretty even, greenish-grey bark and if solitarily grown it can reach a diameter of two metres. With a percentage of 14 %, beech trees are the most common trees in German forests. The fruits of the tree are called beechnuts which are very popular among squirrels as well as wild boars. They are slightly poisonous because of a low content of hydrocyanic acid.

Beechnuts – fruits of the Common Beech (Source: Wikipedia)

Characteristics:

In Germany you can find beech trees on calcareous grounds, mixed with ash and sycamore and sufficient soil humidity. This tree appears in combination with sessile oak on dry sites on brown earth soils in northern Germany. In low and high mountain ranges you find beech trees accompanied by spruce trees and silver fir trees. Beech trees can also grow on shady sites. The oval, tapered leaves are bright light green in April and May, then dark green and in autumn yellow or even reddish.

Wood:

The diffuse-porous wood is ideal for wood turning. It tends to warp heavily during the drying process when used very fresh. A mellowing period is helpful to avoid it. You can also steam the wood and so the wood gets its reddish colour. The heavy and tough wood can be bent very well by using steam and still keeps its shape. Carving beech wood is quite difficult because even as greenwood it is very hard. However you can carve spoons from it. I very much like to use it to turn bowls from. And keep in mind, dried beech wood can barely be cleaved.

Sycamore (Acer Pseudoplatanus)

Sycamore and its companion Norway maple are spread all over Germany, mainly in low mountain ranges. Its sap can be used to win sugar in early spring and with it you can make wine. The bees like to visit its blossoms and produce a qualitatively high-ranked honey. When we were children we liked to stick half of a fruit with its two seeds on our nose and in late summer we let them twirl through the air as propellers. After 120 years the diameter of a tree trunk is approximately 60 centimetres.

Lobed eave edges - Sycamore. (Source: Wikipedia)

Characteristics:

Sycamore is fast-growing in its youth. After ten years is has already reached a height of four metres and has grown quite straight. It is also a pioneer tree. The tips of the Sycamore leaves have round edges on their significant five-lobed leaves. Norway Maple has tapered leave edges instead. The bark is quite even and grey-brown-green.

Wood:

The wood is light and diffuse-porous with a very small amount of heartwood. Annual rings can particularly be seen well on a young tree because at that stage they lay up to a centimetre apart. Sycamore is especially suitable for wood turning and caving kitchen utensils because this wood is completely tasteless and barely has any tannins. And due to this low amount it cannot be used for outdoor areas. Soon after the wood is cut, first brown marks will appear under the bark. After drying the wood is tough and durable.

Little-leaf Linden (Tilia Cordata)

Stories and songs about the linden tree , in certain English-speaking areas also called lime tree, are part of the traditional lore in Germany. Besides oak trees they have an immense meaning for Germany's national identity and stand for loyalty and love for the homeland. Up to one thousand years of age are no problem for a linden tree. The young linden leaves either of the large-leaf linden tree or of the little-leaf linden tree, the second blossoms roughly two weeks later, can be used to prepare a tasty salad and linden honey is also very popular. Tea made of linden blossoms is diaphoretic.

Linden blossom honey tastes fantastically. (Source: Wikipedia)

Characteristics:

Linden trees can reach a height up to 40 metres and as a solitary tree their treetop is widely spread. Their serrated heart-shaped leaves are up to 15 centimetres in size. The leaves of a little-leaf linden tree are significantly smaller – that is an indicator to differ between the species. A trunk diameter up to 1.8 metres is not unusual. Its bark is deeply furrowed. The fruits of a linden tree are small round capsules on a wing-leaf.

Wood:

Linden wood is extremely soft. Therefore it is a preferred wood for carving – the favourite wood of Tilman Riemenschneider. Spoons, ladles and pots are easily to craft from this wood. During drying the originally light wood quickly turns to an orange-reddish colour. It is only suitable for indoor areas because it rots fast. Since ancient times linden bast, which is the inner bark (between outer bark and wood) was used for rope-making. The fibres are resistant and tough therefore they are also used to weave chair seats.

Common Ash (Fraxinus Excelsior)

Yggdrasil, so the world tree in northern mythology was called. It was an ash tree. Ratatöskr, the squirrel, brought on its trunk messages from Asgard via Midgard to Niflheim and back. The ash tree has a high stump regrowth capability. This characteristic makes it a predestined tree for coppicing. An ash tree can reach an age up to 300 years.

Ash trees can grow tall. (Source: Wikipedia)

Characteristics:

Ash trees can grow up to 40 metres in height and the maximum trunk diameter is about five metres. In young years the bark is quite even and light grey, aged it is darker and deeply furrowed. The pinnate ash leaves consist of nine to fifteen paripinnated leaflets (small leaves). The panicle is hardly to recognize but the ripening fruits, which ripen between September and October, are well-visible as dense dark tussocks.

Wood:

Ash wood is less suitable for outdoor areas but it is extremely impact-resistant, hard and tough. Therefore the ring-porous wood is a preferred material to make tool handles or furniture. As green wood it is a fine material for wood turning. In Great Britain bodgers very much like to turn chair legs and other items from it. A haft made of ash wood is a basic standard for hammers, axes and hatchets in Germany. Ash wood provides a high heating value too. So a greenwood worker and a firewood trader compete all the time.

Common Hazel (Corylus Avellana)

Nearly everyone likes to eat hazelnuts and may it only be Nutella, a tasty spread made of hazelnuts. Especially on the edge of forests you find the tall grown shrubs with its many shoots. Every year in May my great-grandfather went behind the house, cut off a branch and used it to make me a whistle. The second one got my grandma, so she could whistle to let all know that lunch was ready. Due to its excellent regrowth capability it is great for coppicing.

Hazel bushes are easy to recognize. (Source: Wikipedia)

Characteristics:

The multi-stem shrub loves summer-warm, bright habitats. Its shoots can reach a height of up to five metres and an age of eighty to one hundred years is likely. If based in coppicing forests its rotation period ranges from seven to ten years. The leaves are velvety and round. The bark is dark brown with small scars. Hazelnuts are food for many small mammals like squirrels.

Wood:

Hazel wood is rather medium hard. You cannot use it in outdoor areas due to its short durability. However hazel rods are used as garden-shaping elements or fences, even as growing and climbing aid. Because of its long-fibred wood and as a result its flexibility it is well-suitable for shafts of gardening tools, e.g. hay rakes. You can make baskets, walking sticks and bows from hazel wood. It is less suitable for wood turning and carving because of its rather small diameter.

Sessile Oak (Quercus Petraea)

German oak trees, mostly sessile oak and common oak, have a similar importance like linden trees in German tradition and customs. I admit, the mighty tree giants, which can grow very old, have a calming effect on me. An oak tree can reach an age of one thousand years. Its fruits are used for pig fattening and wildlife feeding. Bitter substances hinder humans to consume them. However a coffee substitute called "Muckefuck" was made out of it. A pitch black ink is made by using gall nuts, a proliferation on the underside of the leaf caused by fertilized eggs of the gall wasp, and iron sulphate. Even today this ink is used to sign international treaties.

Acorns fatten pigs. (Source: Wikipedia)

Characteristics:

Like any other oak tree the sessile oak has lobed leaves. The bark is even, grey-brown in its youth and deeply-furrowed in age. On stony grounds in low mountain ranges sessile oak trees grow better than common oak trees. Acorns of sessile oaks trees stand in dense tussocks, almost without a stalk on a branch – therefore its name, and can be up to three centimetres long. An oak tree has a good regrowth capability and so it is used for coppicing, especially in areas where the bark is used for tanning purposes.

Wood:

The oak tree is a heartwood tree with nearly no sapwood. The wood is very hard and tough. Because of its richness in tannins it is long-lasting, almost no pests or parasites infest it and even in humid environments it slowly rots. These characteristics allow the use of oak wood in underwater construction and ship building as well as normal construction wood. Basically it is good for all items which are exposed to any effects of the weather. I have made tools, which need to have a certain stability, from oak wood like my rounder plane. But I did not consider that the tannins react with steel. That is the reason axe hafts loosen with time. Beech wood would have been a better choice. Green oak wood can be processed easily but cleaning your tool is highly recommended to save your blades from the effects of the tannins.

Black Alder (Alnus Glutinosa)

Black alder trees prefer wet habitats. So you always find them next to brooks and in bogs. The region "Spreewald" and the surrounding flat areas are densely covered with these trees. Even at the brook sides next to our mill where I grew up, stood alder trees. Neither my great-grandfather nor my father have ever used the wood but I like it very much. In the past the cones were made into ink and the bark was used to tan leather.

Black alder trees often grow on wet grounds. (Source: Wikipedia)

Characteristics:

Alder trees belong to the family Betulacea and disperse by wind. The fruits are small, black woody cones. Alder leaves are round and have no leaf point. These trees can grow for circa 120 years and reach a height of up to 28 metres. The bark is grey-brown and furrowed. Moreover they have a high content of tannins.

Wood:

Alder wood turns into an intense orange colour if it is exposed to air. That allows a nice contrast in combination with other kinds of wood. This wood is used by toy makers. In the Ore Mountains they like to work with alder for hoop turning. Alder wood is used in underwater construction because of its durability. Half the city of Venice stands on alder poles (the other half on oak poles). I carved spoons from it and made branch furniture items. The wood is also great for bowl turning. By the way, do not throw away alder shavings. If your neighbour owns a smoker, he would happily take them to smoke fish and meat.

Fruit Woods (Cherry, Plum, Pear, Apple)

Wood of fruit trees usually is very hard and dense. Therefore you need to process them as greenwood. They are suitable to make any kind of kitchen utensils like spoons, bowls or ladles. Especially plum wood shows a high contrast between heartwood and sapwood and that results in a very nice grain of the wood. Pear and apple wood are short-fibred. It was likely that yarn bobbins were made of pear wood. Never say no if you have the chance to get fruit wood.

Cheery wood is very popular among wood turners. (Source: Wikipedia)

Tools for
the Greenwood Workshop

Without the right tools you cannot operate a greenwood workshop. But do not be afraid because you do not have to invest hundreds of Euros for your basic equipment. Some fundamental tools from a DIY-store are enough to get you started straight away. With these you can make other tools and devices. Later you extend your tool inventory one after another, depending what your aims are. In about two years my humble toolkit has grown to a nearly complete range of tools and devices for my workshop

Buying Tools

Inexpensive sources for tools are local DIY-stores . Here you find basic items like hammers, saws and hatchets. Ebay[2] offers more specific tools. Every now and then you can discover inexpensive historical tools under the menu "antiques and art" – "old professions" – "carpenter" at the German Ebay. Ebay in other countries may have listed them under a different category. In most cases they are offered for decorative purposes. But it is so much more interesting to trace back their original purpose, give them a new life and use them productively.

If you visit your friend's workshop and find in some dark basement corners tools which he might not need, ask him if you can get them.

---

[2] http://www.ebay.de

On flea markets you can also find inexpensive and very good tools.

Specialized shops for wood working tools are rather seldom to find. On the internet I can recommend, without any hesitation, two online-shops with a wide range of high quality tools for the greenwood workshop. Dieter Schmid[3] made himself a good name with his website within Germany and beyond. Dictum[4] is a visual appealing and well-sorted catalogue. Both stores are not that cheap. But still, both are trying to offer less expensive tools in good quality, too.

What do I need?

Your raw material comes as a log. This one is split and cut into the needed length. Then follows a rough shaping. In further steps you get closer to your final product shape by using work steps like drilling, hollowing out, carving and wood turning. The last steps are smoothing the surface and any kind of treatment to enhance the durability of wood. During these work steps the work piece has to be fixed, so that you can work with both hands. And of course you need to mark the shape of your work piece, which makes it much easier to meet the desired shape.

For these work steps you need suitable tools. In the following sections I describe the tools, which you need for the above-mentioned steps. Either you buy them or make them yourself. And at the end of each section I give details on additional tools and devices. These are not absolutely necessary but make work a lot easier.

---

[3] http://www.feinewerkzeuge.de
[4] http://www.dictum.de

Various mallets

Minimum Requirements

Your most essential basic tools are a proper hatchet, a good carving knife, hacksaw, which allows you to saw through logs with up to 30 centimetres diameter and a chopping block, which serves as a base for working with the hatchet. Every log with 30 centimetres in diameter and a height of sixty to seventy centimetres can be used as a chopping block. Best suitable is oak wood because it hardly rots outside. It is also important to have an auger with a big diameter, e.g. 1 ½ inch, that is 3.8 cm in diameter.

You can use it in combination with a brace but that requires some muscle power. Alternatively you find some with a T-handle, which allow you to work with both hands. A wooden mallet which you can make yourself by using hatchet and knife, is helpful too.

Here's a little sketch of a simple mallet and how it's made. A handle diameter of 1 ½" is suitable in size for most hands.

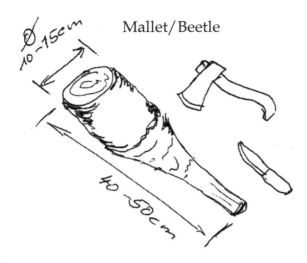

Mallet/Beetle

,

Splitting Wood

A longer log should rather lie on preferably soft ground, e.g. a meadow. Any logs up to one metre length can also be split standing upright. For that procedure you need a hatchet, wedges and a big, heavy wooden hammer. The steel version is called "Bello" in German. With a hatchet you set a starting split and extend it with the wedges until the wood is split at its entire length. Do not hit steel on steel! You only need to buy a hatchet. All the other tools you can make yourself. If you split wood it is not crucial that your hatchet is perfectly sharpened. Basically it is enough if it is reasonably sharp.

Heavy Mallet

For the hammer head you vertically drill with an auger a 3 to 4 cm big hole through the middle of a log with a diameter of 20 cm, circa 15 cm away from the end. Later on the shaft will be fixed here. Then cut the log to a length of 30 cm and so you have your hammer head. For the shaft you need a piece of hazel or ash wood with a slightly bigger diameter than the hole. It should be 0.8 to 1 m long. With a knife you carve the area, where the hammer head will be positioned, to the right diameter. Split the carved end in the middle with a knife on a length of 1 cm and fit the hammer head on it.

Then carve a 3 to 4 cm long and 0.5 cm thick wedge from dried wood in the same width like the hole and by hitting with the back of a hatchet or with a hammer you fix the wedge in the prepared split and so you tighten your hammer head. Watch the direction of the split and wedge in the sketch!

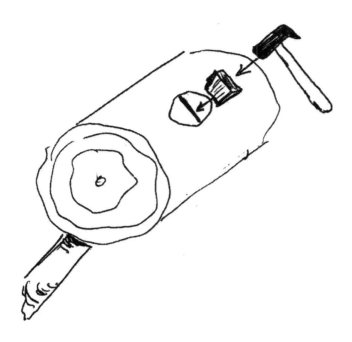

Wedges

For making wedges, hard and short-fibred wood like beech or sycamore is ideal. However oak and chestnut wood function as well without any problems. Even with birch wood I have made good experiences as long as it stored dryly. Branches with a diameter of 6 to 10 cm are well-suitable for wedges. Saw two to three straight pieces of a branch with a length of 30 to 40 cm. Leave 10 to 15 cm and the rest is made into a wedge by using a hatchet on a chopping block. The angle of the wedge should have 20 to 25 degrees.

To reach good results, use the hatchet like in the illustration below.

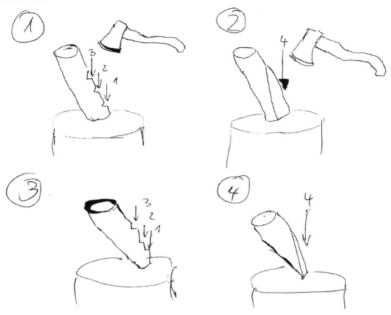

Additional tools

Especially for splitting short (up to 50 cm in length) and rather thin (up to 10 cm in diameter) wood a froe is most suitable. Nowadays historical froes are very rarely to find and are sold for much money on Ebay. New froes cannot be bought in DIY-stores in Germany. In Great Britain or in the USA a froe is easier to obtain. You'll find them sometimes in the hardware stores and in specialized online shops. You need to ask a blacksmith to make such a tool except you intend to want to try it yourself. A solid base is an old leaf spring with 15 to 30 cm length and 3 to 5 mm thick. On it you bent and weld and eye for the shaft or you simply weld it together. The blade itself gets hardened and tempered, so it will be tough and doesn't break under tension.

The bevel on the bottom edge of the blade is single-sided on the right or double-sided in an angle of circa 25 degrees. A froe doesn't have to be very sharp nor does it need to cut. Its purpose is to set the base for splitting wood properly. To that it will only be hewn and the leverage effect splits the wood with better results than the hatchet.

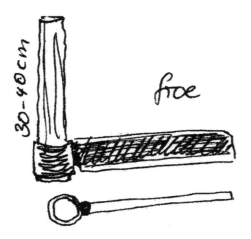

Additional information

For splitting long, thin logs you use a riving brake as an additional device. Here you press the split open with a froe, push further and balance the split by pressing the wood on the right side until the log is centrically split on its complete length.

Images of riving brakes you find via image search of a search engine with the search words "riving brake" and videos about "riving" or "cleaving" are on Youtube. I strongly recommend to watch videos to learn which side of the wood to press to keep the split in the middle.

Riving/Cleaving Brake

Sawing Wood

Sawing generates its effect by cutting the wood fibres. The durability of fibres, in opposite to splitting wood, where it is kept, will be destroyed or at least weakened with cuts through the fibre. But splitting doesn't allow to work sidewise to the grain and you need to cut the wood into the desired length. You sharpen the saw teeth with the help of a fine file, to guarantee its function on the one hand. On the other hand the saw teeth need to stand a little apart to the left and to the right to generate a wider slot, so that the following saw blade runs smoothly and without any friction. This sidewise protruding of the saw teeth is called setting. To cut a log to the needed length you sometimes need to put it onto a sawhorse.

European Saws

Saws in our regions mostly work on pushing it. That means, the biggest material take-off is reached by pushing the saw away from your body. Only the big, by two man operated saws (wedding saw, crosscut saw) for felling or cutting big wood diameters are working with traction. Are you working on your own, a so called one-man crosscut saw replaced the one operated by two people. You get them in shops with a length up to 90 cm. The setting in the end part is so, that you can place your first cut easily. In the main part of the blade usually four teeth alternate with a big gap in between.

You'll find a hacksaw with a metal frame in every DIY-store. It is inexpensive, sturdy and because mostly gardeners are among the customers, these saws have already been equipped with the right blade to cut green wood. On today's saw blades only the teeth are hardened and tempered, recognizable on the bluish coloured teeth row.

Buy a hacksaw in a length of 80 to 90 cm. The height of the frame above the blade indicates the biggest saw-able wood diameter. A disadvantage of simple hacksaws is that the cut often cannot be controlled to go straight through the wood and with increasing saw depth it runs away.

A European and two Japanese saws

Frame or buck saws with a wooden frame, also called carpenter saws, are the typical tool to saw boards and slats very accurately. The tension of the blade, in difference to a hacksaw, is not reached via the frame itself but the blade is rather strained by twisting the tension rope depending on your needs.

For a longer storage without using the saw or for transporting it you should loosen the tension. With a rotating handles on the blade you can adjust the angle between blade and saw frame. With very thin blades with circa 0.5 cm width, which are barely to find in shops, you are able to saw out round shapes.

A backsaw is suitable for cutting small slats. As its name says, it makes very fine cuts. In combination with a mitre box it is unbeatable for perfect angular cuts. The rip saw is also used by a carpenter for cuts of dried wood. Because of the non-existing frame the saw depth is unlimited. The wide blade allows a good handling but a later correction of the direction of a cut is hardly possible. Therefore you should, before you saw valuable items, train your skills in advance.

Japanese Saws

In opposite to European saws Japanese saws work with traction and the meterial take-off happens by pulling the saw towards the body. Meanwhile I prefer this technique. Bigger saws very often have an angled handle but mostly you find saws with a straight handle similar to a shaft. The most important forms are Dozuki, Kataba and Ryoba. A steel back supports the blade of a Dozuki saw. It is especially suitable for fine cuts but the saw depth is limited by the back. The Kataba doesn't have this problem. Without a saw back it has no saw depth limitation. But the blade snaps off relatively fast on back feeding with too much pressure and so you need to work carefully.

I suggest buying a Ryoba. The blade is elongated trapezoidal and toothed on both sides. One side is exclusively for cross cuts of the fibre, the other side cuts along the grain. You will understand fast, which side with its particular setting is used for what kind of cuts, if you use the wrong side by mistake. While working with Japanese saws, take care of a clean cut because similar to a hacksaw, cutting through thin wood does barely allow any corrections of the direction. And, be careful: Because of its double-sided teeth there is a higher risk of injury!

Sawhorses

The hinged sawhorse with crossed legs is standard in Germany. Originally two crosses were used – today three. The third cross supports the use with a chain saw for sawing short pieces of a log for firewood production. I recommend the use of a wooden sawhorse. If a saw slips off and the saw teeth hit the metal, bent teeth and a blunt blade are the result otherwise.

Alternatively I found a fast self-constructed form from Great Britain in F. Lambert's booklet "Tools and Devices for Coppice Crafts". Putting a branch fork upside down in a drill hole of a slightly bent log you construct a stable tripod. Let it protrude from the drill hole of the and you have a stop for the wood which will be sawn. I have figured out that you can cut thinner logs with that kind of sawhorse very well. The making of such a saw horse is shown later in this book.

Additional Saws

To saw something out of your work piece you need a jigsaw. Unfortunately I haven't seen any hand tool in retail. But on Ebay I have come across some old ones which are, with some rework of the setting and teeth sharpening, well usable again. Look for rather narrow saw teeth and little rust.

The sharpening of saws is a science of itself. But you need to re-sharpen the teeth. Today that is barely possible because of the saw teeth are only hardened at the teeth area – especially Japanese saws with their special bevel and their fine teeth setting are made that way. Old saws or modern ones, which are made like old-style saws can be re-sharpened by you. To re-sharpen a saw you need a rhombic file, sometimes even a triangular file works. To set the saw teeth you need a saw tooth setter in a matching size. Again, I wouldn't try sharpening and tooth setting on Japanese saws.

A buck saw used together with a saw horse (Source: Wikipedia)

Rough Shaping

Is the wood cut into length and split to about the right size follows the rough removal of excessive material. In most cases the removal is made from the outside. Far less you have to make hollows. For outside wood removal you need an axe or hatchet. Wikipedia says, that an axe is wielded two-handed and a hatchet single-handed. For hollowing out you can uses an adze. Adzes are available for surface finishing (straight adze) or for hollowing out (bowl adze and gutter adze). In this section I particularly refer to the bowl adze.

Axe

You usually don't need a both-handed axe for greenwood work. The exception is the case, if you actually felled a tree, which you want to process, by hand. The notch, which determines the fall direction of the tree, is hewn with an axe. The rest you can do with a one-man saw or a crosscut saw and a helper. The Rhineland axe head pattern is typical for Germany.

I personally like a head weight of about 1.5 kg. In Britain the Kent head shape is common and US-American axes usually have a more compact head.

Should you intend to work in carpentry and you want to make beams from tree trunks you need a side axe. With it you flatten and straighten the outsides of the trunks. It has only a single-sided bevel and is similar to a side hatchet in its shape but it is bigger, heavier and with a longer shaft. However carpenters are not that fuzzy and use the one they can wield best. From a bearded axe via a goosewing-shape to the Krain pattern from the

Alps region, any pattern is used as long as a carpenter can rely on it.

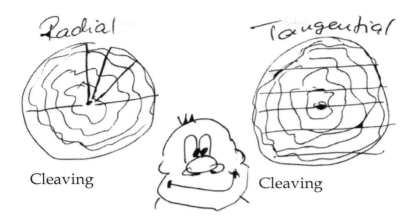

Cleaving   Cleaving

Hatchet

You should take good care and test, which shape you are deciding for. In many cases a greenwood craftsman owns various hatches after a certain time and uses different head shapes for tasks the particular hatchet might be most suitable for. For instance, I prefer the Rhineland pattern with a short shaft to make spoon blanks, a Pakistani hatchet for bowl blanks or a French side hatchet for even surfaces. For the beginning a simple hatchet with 600 to 750 g head weight is adequate and costs 10 to 20 Euro at a DIY-store.

Many spoons carvers swear by the Swedish head shape and the good steel. Well-known brands from Swedish forges are for instance Gränsfors Bruks[5], Wetterlings[6] or Hultafors[7]. And truly the steel of these axes keeps a very good edge, re-sharpen your axe is seldom necessary.

---

5 http://www.gransfors.se
6 http://www.wetterlings.com
7 http://www.hultafors.se

Personally I am not very fond of the small blade of the lighter hatchets. While the small Rhineland pattern edge measures 10 to 12 cm, a Swedish hatchet I own offers only 7 to 8 cm.

Side hatchets are bevelled single-sided and often have a flared shaft.

Special carving hatchets have an extremely upward bent tip, in English also called „toe". A carver mostly works with this part of the blade. Hans Karlsson's forge[8] from Sweden offers such hatchets. My own Pakistani carving axe of Golra Tools[9], is no typical carving axe. On my wish it was modified and is bevelled single-sided and the delivered haft from olive wood I replaced by a self-made birch haft because it fits my hand much better.

---

[8] http://www.hanskarlsson.se
[9] http://www.golratools.com

Small „Bodger"-hatchet with a slightly bent shaft

To work at ease it is interesting and important which shape the haft has. It should not be too big in diameter, especially for women. Try to make and test different shapes and thicknesses of hafts yourself. Examples for it can be found on the internet. The most suitable material for hafts in our region is ash wood.

For lighter hatchets, which have to take lower power impact, even birch wood is possible. Important is the long-fibrousness of wood. Oak wood is less suitable for the haft of steel tools. The content of tannins of the wood is too high - it reacts chemically with steel after a certain time and the head become loose.

I recommend besides buying a simple 600 g hatchet from a DIY-store also the purchase of a side hatchet, also called carpenter's hatchet. Currently the prices on eBay for such a hatchet in good condition are between 40 to 60 Euros. It has a completely flat side and a single-bevel a sidewise bent shaft is most characteristic. This serves protecting your knuckles if you work closely with wood. Side hatchets are available for right and left handed people.

Adze

The adze, in German called "Dechsel" – occasionally also "Dexel" or "Texel", is one of the oldest tools of mankind. In difference to a hatchet the blade is twistedly fixed by 90° and therefore is also called an "across axe". Is the blade straight, than it is called a flat adze and if it is convex it is a bowl adze. Bowl adzes are nearly unbeatable for hollowing out wood. Mould makers and coopers used them very often. Wooden gutters or water pipes were made by this tool too but a gutter adze would be an even better choice in this case. Depending on its intended purpose, size, weight or width, bend and the radius of the blade (the sweep) are very different.

Greenwood workers mostly use the bowl adze to hew and carve bowls. According to the intended size of the bowl adzes with a width of 2 to 4 cm are used. It's hard to find an inexpensive adze that size in Germany you can only get them at flea markets where the seller doesn't have any idea of the value of the tool. Adzes are hardly to find in shops here. I only know of two specialized German internet-traders (Dictum[10], Dieter Schmid[11]), who offer adzes. And only Dictum produces them themselves.

---

[10] http://www.dictum.de
[11] http://www.feinewerkzeuge.de

Small 2.5 cm adze of a Bulgarian smith

But if you look internationally, using the English term „adze" with a search engine, you'll find good offers. My own 450 g adze with circa 1 inch blade width comes from a Bulgarian blacksmith. Best quality you get from Swedish and British forges like Hans Karlsson or Nick Westermann[12], but it has its price. An adze of comparable size to mine, which cost circa 25 Euros, costs at that place 90 Euros or more.

Additional tools

Coppicing is, in comparison to Britain, rather seldom to find in Germany (in German it is called „Niederwaldwirtschaft "). Hazel, sycamore, ash, oak or trees and scrubs with a good regrowth capability are cut down (to the stump) every seven to twenty

---

[12] http://www.nickwestermann.co.uk

years in a rotary system, then they sprout again and grow another period of time. In regions, where oak bark was used for tanning or on stone ridges in the Ore Mountains you can still find this kind of forest management.

In short rotation coppice thin material, up to a diameter of 5cm like hazel or shrubs, is traditionally cut with a billhook (in German also called "Gertel"). In a good DIY-store in Germany you find this as Swiss Gertel for about 30 to 40 Euros. If you cannot befriend with this pattern, you can find the "billhook" in the most versatile patterns at any British tool traders starting at about 25 British Pound.

Fine Shaping

Fine shaping removes rough humps and dents, which were left over during the previous work step and it brings the work piece to its required measurement and the desired shape. In doing so, you use very different tools and devices.

All Kinds of Knives

Drawknife and spoke shave

For work on a shaving horse, whose construction I am going to explain in the section clamping devices, you need a drawknife. You hold it both-handed and draw it during the wood removal towards you. Here exist most different shapes and versions. For normal work I recommend a drawknife with a 20 to 25 cm long blade. Straight drawknives with long handles are very often to find in Great Britain. Because handle and blade are often at the same level, it doesn't matter if you do the work from top or bottom of the drawknife – try which way you can work well with it. German drawknives have a slight bend towards you in the blade and the handles are below the cutting level. That fact determines that the bevel must show upwards, otherwise work is nearly not possible. Drawknives with such a convex blade are mostly easier to work with but they are by far more aggressive in chip removal than straight knives. Be careful here.

The small version of a drawknife is a spoke shave. It is used for the remaining very fine shavings which need to be removed from the surface. It consists of a body and a knife. Best well-known are spoke shaves with a metal body. Here the blade is similar to a plane iron and is fixed with a screw. More expensive versions even have two adjusting screws for fine adjustment. Traditional versions of spoke shaves consist of a wooden body which is made of boxwood or beech wood. The knife is put via a sole into two holes and is fixed at the needed height, usually 0.2 – 0.5 mm, by tapping. The distance between knife and wooden body determines the thickness of the wood chips. This shape of a tool had already been proven by findings during excavations in Novgorod.

A normal, straight carving knife with a circa 10 cm long blade belongs to the basic equipment of a greenwood worker. For easier sharpening I recommend a blade made of carbon steel. Very good knives, which almost have become standard, are produced by the Swedish company Mora[13]. They are available throughout Germany and cost 20 to 30 Euros. Their blades are 3 mm wide and consist of laminated steel (hard blade between two softer elastic steel layers). Alternatively I recommend carving knives of the

---

13 http://www.moraknives.com

Pakistani forge Golra Tools. They are only 2 mm thick and made all in all of carbon steel.

Spoon Knives

Straight knives, two spoon knives and a small push knife

To cut hollows into wood you need a bent knife – the spoon knife or crooked or hook knife. However, the name might refer to spoons, you use it for all hollowing, even little bowls and cups. A manufacturer of inexpensive spoon knives is Mora once more. Users often argue about the usability of these knives. I own a Mora 164 (bevelled one-sided, small radius) and a 163 (bevelled both-sided, big radius). I very much like to work with variant 164 because here, in opposite to double-sided bevels, you can use the thumb for support. For spoon knives there are many manufacturers in the most versatile price categories and qualities. Do you search in Google for a "crooked knife" or a "hook knife", you will find some very quickly all around the globe.

A second variant had a blade shaped like a ring. This has an advantage for you because there is no need to turn the work piece if the fibre direction changes. If the blade is at least half a circle or more, so the specific term for it is Scorp. Such scorps have ever been known since time. So some examples were found during excavations in Novgorod. I own a replica for larger bowls of the discovered one in Novgorod. Such a replica you can get at the museum shop of the history park Bärnau[14]. Another smaller scorp I got from the British blacksmith Richard Douglass, who you can only find on Facebook[15]. It has a one inch diameter and it is my preferred tool for carving spoons.

Drilling

To get holes in your work piece you need a drilling machine and a drill. Let us start with big diameters and successively we work towards small ones. Really big holes are made with hand augers. The handle of the auger is fixed in T-shape, so that you can work both-handed. However, two shapes of augers exist. One, similar to a long small shell or slug house, is tapered to the bottom. This shape is used to drill holes along the grain. The blade works from a small towards a big diameter and with a lead screw it pulls itself through the wood.

The other shape with two horizontal blades at the bottom drills the desired diameter instantly and is similar to a spiral after the blades, which serves chip transport and the guidance of the drill. With this shape you drill across the grain. Both variants you only should buy with a diameter bigger than 1 inch. For smaller

---

[14] http://www.geschichtspark.de
[15] http://www.facebook.de

diameters you don't need so much power of the T-handle. Available online are mostly historic tools or remaining stocks of the German Federal Army. A search on America Ebay is successful by entering „barn auger".

Brace and auger

For diameters up to 1.5 inch you use a brace and an appropriate auger. If you like to own a used historic brace, take care of the chuck on your purchase. The jaws, which grab the drill on its shaft, should be undamaged and not bent. Braces with two or four jaws in the chuck are normal. Take also care of the square inside the chuck – it should not be worn out.

Modern augers for the brace only have one blade and a hexagonal shaft for clamping. If you want to clamp them into the brace you need a chuck with three jaws or an adapter to the old square – available i.e. at Dictum. But I recommend finding old drills at a flea market or on Ebay. They are designed for manual work and with reference to my experience they are easier to work with than modern augers. Useful sizes, often stated in inch – here metric, are 8mm, 10mm, 12mm, 14mm, 16mm, 18mm, 20mm, 25mm and 32mm.

Small diameters you can either drill with a gimlet (available at DIY-stores) or more convenient with a breast drilling machine and the usual spiral drills for wood or metal up to a 10mm diameter. Good hand powered drilling machines mostly have two gears by having two different cogwheels in size. You change the gear by re-plugging the crank. So you drill more slowly in the first gear but transfer more power via the crank to the bigger drill diameter – like in a car. Hand drills can be bought either on Ebay or at internet-traders.

Spindle Turning

Spindle turning is the relatively easy start to greenwood turning. Even the tools are available straight away. These are standard wood turning tools. You need at least three of them: a wide gouge, a wide straight chisel and a small turning gouge. With the wide gouge you turn the work piece round. It needs to endure a lot. Provided with one inch width, better two inches, and a long handle, it serves you well. The inexpensive start is a 2.5 cm gouge from the DIY-store, which you can give a long handle on your own.

The straight wood chisel should also be wide if possible. It serves for flattening and smoothing the surface and for giving it the right shape. Here a shorter handle is often enough. An authentic wood turning chisel has a double-sided angular bevel. It's called a skew chisel. I personally like to work with a normal, 4 cm wide firmer chisel. The small turning gouge should be 12 mm wide with a fingernail-shaped bevel. In general you should check the angle of the bevel for an easier work. On power turning machines the dry wood is scraped during wood turning, when greenwood turning you cut it. So the angle must be different. It must be smaller for a sharper tool for freshly cut wood. It should be 20 to 25 degrees.

Bowl Turning

Opposite to spindle turning there are no ready manufactured tools for bowl turning in Germany. You need to forge the so-called hook tools yourself, ask a local blacksmith or order them in Great Britain, for instance at Ben Orford[16]. Two or three of these tools are enough for most tasks. I recommend a double-bevelled hook with outside grind, one double-bevelled hook with inside grind and eventually, if you intend to turn nested bowls, a bent hook, which provides you the curve for the outer bowl shape of the nested ones.

Scorps in different sizes

---

[16] http://www.benorford.co.uk

Further Tools

The Scorp doesn't only exist in small diameters, but also coopers and mould makers use big Scorps up to a diameter of 15 cm. They are led both-handed like a drawknife. With big surfaces you smooth surfaces of hollows of hewn-in bowls. Replicas of the medieval original are available at the museum shop of the history park Bärnau. Even the company Pfeil[17] has one to offer. On Ebay you often find old versions.

For wood turning on a pole lathe you need a lathe. Two options differ in weight and shape of the poles. You turn chair legs with the fibre of wood, along its direction of growth, therefore it is called spindle turning. Bowls instead you turn against the fibre, thus called bowl turning. Because bowl blanks very often have a noticeable imbalance and partially have a very wide diameter, the lathe needs to be heavier to compensate vibrations.

---

[17] http://www.pfeil-tools.ch

Sanding

My experience with users of my products tells me that women like smooth sanded surfaces on spoons or bowls, while men rather prefer the more raw, hand-carved and turned versions, because these are more rustic. Sanding is boring but sometimes necessary. Due to that here you find a small overview about everything you might need.

Electrical sanding Devices

Sometimes you'll have to work with dried boards, like for a seat of a shaving horse or for chopping boards in the kitchen. Depending on the quality of the wood (construction wood or carpenter's quality) the surface varies. I remove the rough cuts of the saw by using an orbital sander. Because you might not sand a whole square metre, a semi-professional device with 105 mm disc diameter will do perfectly. In addition I use a delta shaped sander with fine sandpaper to reach small corners and cavities.

Sanding Paper

Sanding paper you can find in the most different versions at every DIY-story: for wood, for metal, combined, for wet or dry sanding. By the way you only sand wood when dried and always in direction of the fibre. I sometimes make a small exception but only if the wood is nearly dry. The difference is in the grit – the coarseness of sanding paper. The smaller the grit the more coarse is the surface. While sanding you start with coarse sandpaper (grit 80) followed by the grits 120, 240 and 400. I stop usually here. Really well sanded surfaces can be reached with grit of 600 or more.

Scrapers

An alternative to sanding is surface processing with scrapers. You get them, mostly in a set, at a good tool trader. Straight edges, with convex and concave curves and a shape, which is called swan neck, are typical. You "sharpen" scrapers with a burnisher, similar to a blade sharpener in kitchens. It gets horizontally dragged over the edge and results in a small burr which then scrapes the wooden surface. The swan neck I often use for bowls and spoons. Mostly you can simply use a knife's blade which you set vertically and start scraping: a fast result, but you need to sharpen the knife more often.

Sharpening Tools

An advice in advance: Take your time to sharpen your tools. Don't rush, so that your hands remember the right angle, the needed pressure or the most effective direction of motion. Only that way you get really sharp blades. Sharpening has always been a science of itself and every craftsman owns his secret recipe, which he swears on and I can admit this too. Just like with sanding and smoothing wooden surfaces you work from coarse to fine grit on the edge of your tool. The grit of sharpening stones is usually not comparable with the grit of sanding paper. Coarse – medium – fine – extra fine comply the grits 300 – 800 – 1200 and 1600. Additionally you need to consider, if you sharpen straight or round blades, if the bevel is inside or outside and what quality you need to reach – for raw work you don't really need a mirror finish on the edge.

Straight sharpening Stones (Whetstones)

Sharpening tools

Basically you differ between water and oil stones. The liquid washes away any abraded metal particles from the pores of the sharpening stone. I prefer water stones, where I don't have to use additional oil. Such sharpening stones exist naturally or are manufactured industrially, mostly made of corundum. Well-known natural stones are Belgian Blue whetstones, a water stone, or the Arkansas whetstone, an oil stone. The finish of my own sharpening tasks is mostly made by a Rozsutec stone from Slovakian sedimentary rock.

Corundum, modified aluminium oxide, has an excellent abrasion during sharpening. Japanese whetstones, made of this material, are one example for good sharpening results. A well-known, inexpensive manufacturer is Sun Tiger, whose 1000/1600 combined stone I like to recommend. Because it permanently lies in water and the grinding sludge is brown, there will be a lot of dirt on your hands while sharpening.

I personally prefer diamond whetstones, which can be used dry or with water. You get an inexpensive set with 150, 300 and 400 grits at every DIY-store. It is more difficult (and mostly more expensive) to buy medium or fine grits. For this I use a foldable pocket grinder. The company Silverline offers an inexpensive double-sided one with 600/1200 grits. By far more expensive are pocket grinders of the USA based company DMT with 1200/6000 grits.

I precede the following way: First I take away coarse notches (grit 150), followed by grit 300 and afterwards I finish simple chopping hatchets with grit 600, grit 1200 I use for cranked hooks for bowls, all knives and blades, which are used for finishing surfaces are sharpened with the Rozsutec-stone with about a 8000 grit.

Special Shapes of grinding Stones

The big whetstones are very suitable for straight blades, like those of chisels, planes and knives. But what is to do, if you want to sharpen spoon knives or a cranked hook. Here you hold the tool tight in your hand and move the stone along the round blades. It is even better, if the grinding stone has the ideal shape. There are bigger stones in drop shape, sticks with different diameters, half-round and triangular shapes.

Round blades with an inside bevel, like some spoon knives and adzes, you sharpen with a little trick. In shops you get wet-dry-sanding paper. Buy sheets with 400, 600 and 1000 grits. Wrap them tightly around a wooden stick with a suitable diameter and you get an excellent substitute for a grind stone. You sharpen round blades with turning the tool and drawing or pulling movements of the sharpening device simultaneously. This trick also works for straight blades if you don't want to invest a lot of money into sharpening gear. Glue the different wet/dry paper grits on boards and you have inexpensive sharpening stone replacements.

Stropping for Mirror Finish

The smoother the blade is, the better the quality of the resulting wooden surface. All carving knives, all chisels (even turning ~), drawknives, carving hatchets or adzes need at least on one side, there where the wood is clinging to, a polished bevel. You reach that with a leather strop and a stropping compound. Leather glued around a stick (for inside bevels) and leather on a circa 6 cm wide x 25 cm long small board with a handle will serve that purpose well. The compound is available in different grits at Dictum or Dieter Schmidt. I use the medium one and I am very satisfied with it. Alternatively, if you spare the investment, any other polish for metal is working, too. I good experiences with a polish for glass ceramic hobs, with scouring agents and the East-German Elsterglanz (a metal polish– translated 1:1 "magpie gloss"). Autosol is widely known in English speaking countries, it works also great.

Leather, raw side up, glued to a board

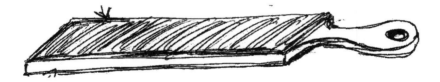

a strop

Treating Surfaces

To make something water proof, to bring colour to the wood and to make everything shiny you need to treat the surface of the finished work piece. Properly treated, the potential user enjoys your work for a long time.

Colouring

Especially in northern Europe colourful wooden kitchen wares are well-known. Swedes and Norwegians paint many of their daily utensils. The first possibility is standard acrylic paint. Alternatively, you can also get oil colour at stationary shops or art supplies shops. But acrylic colour dries within a few hours whereas oil colour needs several weeks. Milk paint colour (with pigments) works well, too. You can extract the casein from curd cheese or you simply buy the ready-made powdery base at a trader. The Kalkladen[18] in Germany offers it.

For precipitation of the powdery casein base you use marble pit lime (paint lasts up to a week in the fridge) or Borax (poisonous, lasts several weeks). Let the mix with water stand overnight. Mix a little of the liquid with the pigments, e.g. soil pigments are totally non-poisonous, und let it soak for two to three hours. Dilute the pigments like needed so that the milk paint colour reaches the saturation you want to achieve after two or three coatings.

---

[18] http://www.kalkladen.de

Oiling

To seal a surface, milk paint colour will do. No colouring you reach by boiling wood in milk for approximately 30 minutes. This treatment is barely suitable for outside areas. I use linseed oil for oiling surfaces nearly all the time. It is a) made from locally grown plants, b) smells good (subjective) and is quite inexpensive and c) cures (hardens) after some time (up to six months). You can purchase linseed oil in bulk packs at horse food traders[19]. So I put spoons and bowls in oil and let them soak for up to 48 hours. Chairs and stools I paint up to five times with it.

But notice, not everyone likes the taste of linseed oil. Bowl and spoons have a little aftertaste. Alternatively use walnut oil. Linseed oil is possible for outdoor areas but it decomposes slowly in direct sunlight. More suitable is mineral oil in this case, e.g. teak oil. It smells nice and seals the surface well.

Bees Wax

Besides oiling also the waxing of surfaces is common. For that you can take bees wax. You get it in granular form on Amazon or at your local beekeeper. Heat and liquefy it and rub it with a cloth on the surface. Then it is shiny, has a pleasant smell and the surface feels velvety. Bees wax is nearly tasteless. Should there be small cracks in the wood, bees wax seals them well like i.e. on the bottoms of shrink pots. And so it can be used for cold liquids without hesitation. But bee wax resolves by adding hot liquids.

---

[19] http://www.meinpferd.de

Clamping Devices

In many cases the difficulty in a greenwood workshop is that you somehow need to fix a rather bulky piece of wood so that you can use both hands to work with a tool. Certainly it can be fixed between the knees quite securely but often this is not enough. For these cases the following section gives you some advice.

Wedges

The easiest way is to wedge a work piece. I use this solution with my bowl horse. I describe its construction in the next chapter. Mostly I use two wedges which I drive in against each other on opposite sides. For that the angle of a wedge is small. I suppose, because I made the wedges myself with a hatchet and without any markings, the angle is about 15°.

Clamp

You should have at least two clamps of different sizes at hand in your workshop. You move the adjustable jaw on the guide rail until it touches the work piece and with the tightening of the screw and increased pressure you clamp it. Does the work piece have straight contact areas on both sides there won't be any problems. Tip: For clamping a log, a clamp together with a sawn out angled piece of wood is helpful to avoid the clamp slipping off of the round wood. At the same time it holds the work piece better because pressure comes from three sides.

Be careful with the surface of the work piece. Sometimes you have to lay paper, a shaving or even an off cut of a board between the clamps jaw and the wood to prevent pressure marks. You get clamps at every DIY-store. Old, sturdy and big clamps are inexpensively available at the flea market.

Holdfasts

The holdfast wedges itself by driving it into a hole in the workbench and so the work piece gets pressed down tightly.

Holdfast

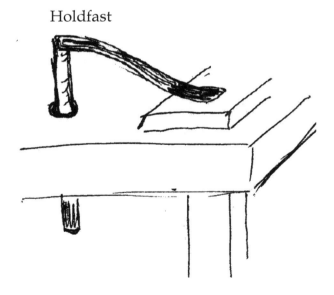

Originally these were supportive tools for fixing work pieces on a bench for planing, back then when vices with bench dogs were not so common. Jacques Roubo introduced the holdfast in his book „L'art de Menusier" from the 18th century. Nowadays you get these helpers extremely rarely. I only know Dictum on the German internet. They offer quite inexpensive holdfasts from Taiwan. Hand-forged versions cost a small fortune. Also with a holdfast the described clamping tip above works excellently. Again, take care while working with clamps or holdfasts that the finished surface of a work piece is protected by inserting a piece of wood in between.

Shaving Horse

Shaving horses are the joiner's work bench of the poor man. By pressure of your feet the work piece is clamped via a lever system and you can work both-handed with a drawknife or a spoke shave. I would like to introduce two different kinds. The English version, which was developed by bodgers, particularly serves the comfortable work with logs. A notch in the pinch roller holds it straight. In particular two lever arms left and right of the seat are used and the rotation axis goes through the seat. The more common version in continental Europe only uses one lever arm which goes through the seat vertically. A horizontal head is responsible for clamping. This dumb-head shaving horse holds flat material like shingles better. It is also known as "shingle horse" in the alp region. Other translated common German names are "Cobold Bench" or "Carving bench". I describe the construction of such a shaving horse in this book.

Work Bench

Mostly a work bench is the starting point of your work – either a heavy and fixed one in the workshop or a lightweight and mobile one on the road. I made my first work benches from DIY-store material (pine, sawn timber). They stand safely and serve you well with a screwed-on vice and adequate loading for mass (I store my steel parts under my workbench for more mass). While working with wood it is advisable to use a wooden vice which doesn't damage the surface and it doesn't react like steel in combination with tannins which results in colour changes.

A new joiner's bench is expensive. Only light-weight models, which are not suitable for a lot of projects, are available at affordable prices. Therefore I show you in this book the construction of a portable work bench, where you only have to invest a little time, besides holdfasts, and a bench screw. It has a leg vice, which was also described in Jacques Roubo's book. It serves you well and it is quite easy to construct. But should you have the chance to get a well-preserved joiner's bench from a joiner's clearance or a sloyd teaching room in schools, use the opportunity and take it.

Measuring and Marking

Carpenter pencils are nice. You can sharpen them simply with a carving knife instead of the always untraceable pencil sharpener. In 90% of all cases they are sufficient for markings on your work piece. A regular pencil you only need in exceptional cases because with it you can get into small holes. Should you need to mark the right drilling depth on your drill, a permanent marker serves you well.

Aids and appliances for measuring and marking

You need a 2 m yard stick (pocket rule, folding ruler) so that your markings make sense. In addition it is necessary to have a try square. Versions in steel or aluminium you get at the DIY-store. It is more difficult to find a wooden one. You only scribe with a divider. To better see it, you trace its line with a pencil. Metal dividers and historical wooden versions with iron tips and mountings are known. The first mentioned metal dividers you find at DIY-stores and the wooden ones I occasionally see on Ebay.

Not to forget a protractor. Do you want to drill the seat of a three-legged stool you need to comply with a 120° angle for an even distribution of holes on the circle. The stool leg should also stand angled (60-75°) for a better sitting stability. Because a protractor doesn't hang in the air, you need a sliding T bevel. With it you adjust the drill. Both devices are also available at the DIY-store.

Building Tools for the Workshop

Now we are getting started with setting up your workshop. I try to guide you through this procedure by including illustrated step-by-step instructions. I always take into account the simple disassembly of the devices for transport. In a shed, the garage or a barn behind the house they are kept dry but it is really fun to bring them into the midst of a forest, set them up and then enjoy your hobby in the middle of nature. Normally I can manage to fit my complete woodturning workshop plus material (in case of a forest as workplace not necessary) in my medium-sized van. Surely the car then has a draught, which you need to have in mind while driving on forest paths, but in most cases I arrive safely at my destination.

By checking the material lists for the projects you will notice that I speak of "circa"-measurements. In greenwood working it is very often not necessary to work accurately and fixed on a millimetre. My measurements should allow a sufficiently good stability of the constructed tools and devices.

Getting milled Timber

You need boards, planks, squared timber and laths to construct your greenwood workshop. The local DIY-store is, of course, a reliable source and you can also buy small amounts but mostly the sawn timber is overpriced there. I suggest that you look for milled timber from a wood trader who delivers to construction companies and joineries. On the one hand he also offers large dimensions and hard wood, which you usually don't find at a DIY-store. On the other hand it's mostly less expensive than in a DIY-store.

Even old wood you should not despise. If an old house near you is demolished, a barn is rebuilt or you find bulky waste on the roadside then you will find quite useful parts in most cases. Certainly the quality may differ a lot. You very often have to remove iron mountings and nails before processing. But also check that the wood doesn't have any rotten spots or if it is glue laminated timber because that one loses its stability quite fast in the open air. With the reuse of old wood you do something good for the environment, because the before invested energy and work is not simply wasted or gets up in smoke.

Getting Greenwood

It is not that easy to get fresh wood in shops. If you are a woodland owner, skip this section but for the rest of mankind getting green wood is very often a problem. Your first source are friends, neighbours and relatives with a property or a garden. Wood always accumulates there. Either landscape gardeners or tree surgeons are your second starting point. They sometimes sell or even give away wood for free when they have to pay money to dispose it.

Responsible for the forest near you are the local forest offices. You can ask here for the price to cut wood yourself or buy freshly felled trees. Even at your local municipal administration there is sometimes wood due to cutting free of paths and the care of parks and also the local construction yard is a further source. Road maintenance depots are responsible for the road network of country and state. Especially after storms or thunderstorms you should enquire. Even energy companies need to keep their transmission lines clear of branches and fell disturbing trees. Normally trees are felled in autumn or winter. Listen like me, when I stroll through my home town, if you can hear the sound of a chain saw. There you often find greenwood if you ask nicely.

Saw Horse and Shaving Horses

You are already able to do some more demanding work with your minimum equipment of tools. But particularly for constructing a shaving horse you need further tools and devices like a chisel and eventually a cordless screwdriver. All for the project used tools and material are summarized in a grey-highlighted box. Saw horse and shaving horse are among the most essential devices which you use in the greenwood workshop. Therefore we start with both of them.

Constructing a Saw Horse

Used Tools

Chopping block (possibly)
Hacksaw/ Japanese saw
1 ½ inch/3.8 cm drill (brace)
Hatchet
Carving knife

Material

Big branch fork with ~ 5 to 8 cm diameter wood, log length: 0.5 m, branch length: 0.5m
Slightly bent log with ~ 10 cm diameter and 1.5 m length

Working Steps

1. Sawing the Log to Length

The bent log needs a length of circa 1.5 m. Leave the bent part and cut the wood on the straight end to length. The bent end will be one of the three supporting feet. Remove any existing twigs with the hatchet. If you chop along growth direction on the log you avoid tearing out the wood.

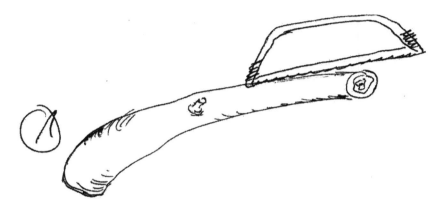

2. Sawing the Branch Fork to Length

A working height of approximately 80 cm is useful for a saw horse. Because the bent log is fixed with a protruding tenon, the branch fork should, if standing on the two branches, be roughly 1 m in height. Therefore take the forking as the midst and cut it to length, 50 cm to the top and 5 0 cm to the bottom. If the branch fork stands on the two branches, the log end should stand vertically on top. Both branches will be the supporting feet of the saw horse. There's an unwritten rule: With three legs everything is standing safe.

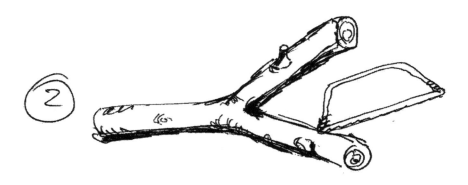

3. Drilling a hole into the log

A tenon on the upper end of the branch fork should go through the log. Therefore drill a hole, approximately 25 to 30 cm away from the end, into straight end of the log. The direction is determined by the bent end. It must point downwards.

Put the fork vertically aside and hold the branch end at about 80 cm height and draw a vertical line for the right angle of the hole. Then you can drill the hole through the middle of the log's straight end.

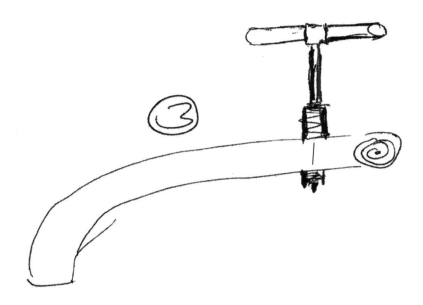

4. Setting the branch fork tenon to diameter

The branch fork needs to be inserted into the just-now-made borehole, so that you get a stable tripod and the protruding tenon serves you as stop for wood you intend to saw. You bring the upwards-showing end of the branch fork to the correct diameter by sawing in around the whole log circa 25-30 cm from the top. Please work carefully here and in small steps!

Afterwards split off the sawn wood from above with the hatchet. Set your hatchet properly and hit with a mallet (as shown before).

Do not use a steel hammer for hitting! When steel hits steel it often happens, that splinter chip off and this can cause unpleasant injuries.

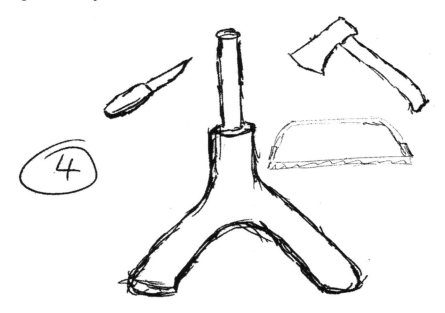

IIf you have reached about 4 cm diameter for the tenon , use only your carving knife until the tenon fits without any big efforts into the hole of the log and the log lies firmly on the sawn section.

Result

The use of the saw horse is simple. Put it together and stand it on a solid base. It can stand nearly everywhere because of its three legs. You press the wood, which you need to saw, against the protruding tenon end and you can start sawing.

Result:

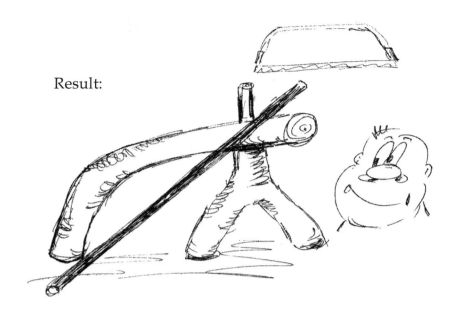

My own saw horse I made by using this method is not that good because I didn't take all work steps into account. My working height is too low on the one hand. It is only 65 cm high. On the other hand I cut my fork branch to short, so I need to plug in an additional round piece of wood which serves as stop. Still, the device is due to its disassembly simple and space-saving and I can work well with it.

Constructing a Shaving Horse

The shaving horse is one of the essential devices in a greenwood workshop. At the same time it is one of the bigger projects, which a greenwood worker has to deal with. And exactly that we want to build now. Besides your basic tools and devices you need a few more tools from the following list, which you can borrow, or, if needed afterwards, buy permanently right away.

Used tools

Hacksaw/Japanese saw, possibly a jigsaw
1 ½ inch/3.8 cm drill (brace)
¾ inch/1.9 cm drill (brace)
½ inch/1.27 cm drill (brace)
Pre-drill 6 mm, possibly with a cordless drill
Hatchet & carving knife
Chisel 1 inch/2.5 cm & mallet
Vice, clamp, board to place underneath
Coarse thread screws (6 - 8 cm long) and cordless screwdriver
Try square
Sliding T bevel (possibly)

Material

Board/plank circa 2.50 m long, ~ 25 cm wide and 5 cm thick
Squared timber circa 6 x 8 cm,~ 1.50 m long
Straight branch wood (e.g. hazel) 5 cm diameter, all in all 2 m
Straight branch wood 2 cm diameter, all in all circa 1.50 m

Working Steps

1. Sawing the Components to Length

Use your newly constructed saw horse straight away to bring the boards and poles to length. You need the following items:
- planks in sizes of 1.5 m, 50 cm, 25 cm and 15 cm length
- branch wood with 5 cm diameter – three items á 55 cm and one circa 10 cm long
- squared timber – one item 50 cm long (enough for now)
- branch wood with 2 cm diameter – one item 30 cm (enough for now)

2. Screwing the Seat together

Screw three to four screws (pre-drill holes in plank) to the end of the 1.5 m long seat piece and fix the 50 cm long squared timber centrically. Here the back legs will be fixed. The wider site of the square timber shows towards the plank. Use a clamp to fix the squared timber centric and in 90° angle to the seat.

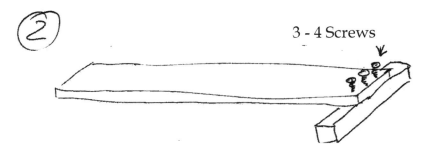

3 - 4 Screws

3. Inserting Legs

Carve with hatchet and knife the three 55 cm long pieces of the 5 cm pole wood at length of 6 – 7 cm to the same diameter like the big drill with 1 ½ inch / 3.8 cm. These will be the tenons of the legs which are inserted in the horse. Drill centrically and in direction of growth with always a distance of 10 cm from the end of plank and squared timber in an angle of 20 – 25° from top through plank and squared timber like shown in the sketch. While drilling clamp an additional board underneath to avoid the fraying of the borehole.

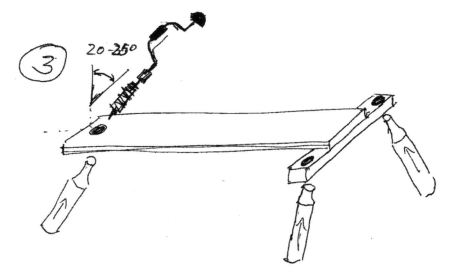

Insert the legs in the boreholes from bottom side. Probably you need to do some extra work on the tenons with the knife. Most probably it's not horizontal by now. We eliminate that in the next step. The tenons will also shrink while drying. Cut them even from top is done when they are dried completely.

4. Setting the Legs to Height

Place your horse on horizontal ground. Start with adjusting the rear end with the two legs. Measure the height from the ground and shorten the longer leg by cutting off the difference. Be aware, because of the underneath screwed squared timber the rear end stands a little higher and you have to cut off more there.

So begin with the front leg. Measure the height from front and rear and finally cut the rear legs to the needed size. It's not too much of a problem when the seat is not 100% horizontal.

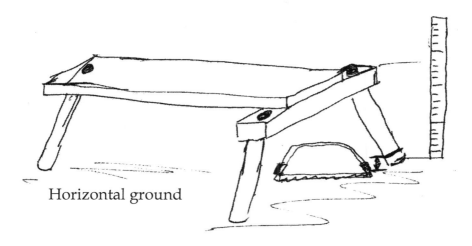

Horizontal ground

5. Preparing the Material Support Area

Because the material support area is, besides the lever, the most important and complex part of the shaving horse, a drawing in advance shows you the final result:

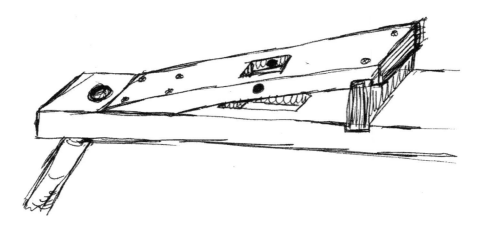

The most difficult task is the sawing of the bevel which shows towards the front leg. A Japanese saw serves you well, because its cut barely runs away from the once pre-set direction. In trouble you can use a rasp to do further adjustments. The vertical, dark-crosshatched small board is the 15 cm long plank. It is set into the seat and the material support area by 1 cm in depth and 3 cm away from the rear end of the material support area. That makes 13 cm distance between horse and lower side of the material support area. By help of the laws of nature of a right-angled triangle you can now construct and saw the bevel. You make the groove on the same side like the bevel for inserting the small vertical board. Use the width of the plank for marking in a 3 cm distance from the end of the material support area. Then saw 1 cm deep into both lines and use the chisel from both sides to create the groove.

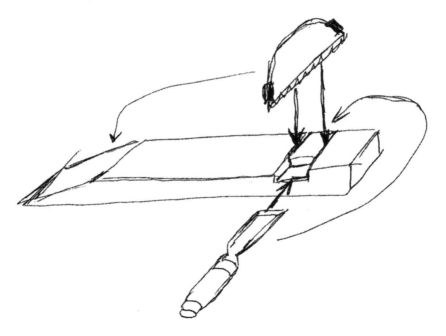

By now the holes for lever and a crossway borehole are missing. Mark the centre of the material support area from the upper side.

Draw symmetrically around it a rectangle of 6 x 12 cm. This will be your slot for the lever arm. If you work with a jigsaw, drill four ½ inch / 1.27 cm holes into the corners, if you work with a chisel, drill as many holes as possible inside the marked rectangle. The jigsaw finishes work quite fast. With a chisel you have more work and you need to chisel from both sides for neat edges. Afterwards extend the centre line to the sides of the material support area and drill a horizontal hole from both sides towards the slot for the lever arm. There the rotation axis of the lever will be put through.

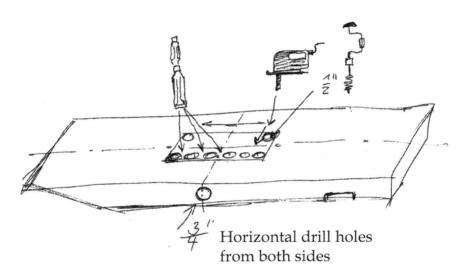

Horizontal drill holes from both sides

6. Preparing the Seat

The centre of the slot for the lever arm lies roughly 37 cm away from the front edge of the horse on the lengthwise centre line. Because the lever arm has a longer way from below, the slot in the seat needs to be longer than the one in the material support area. Construct symmetrically around the slot's centre on the seat a rectangle of 6 cm width and 20 cm length. You do this the same way like described in work step 5.

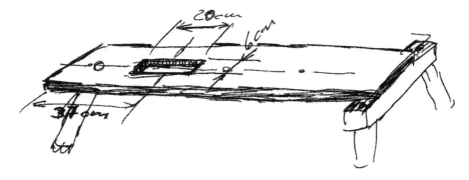

7. Groove in the vertical Plank of the Seat

Like the material support area the seat needs a groove to fit in the short vertical plank. Constructing the groove would be to exhausting. But we can use the measurements of a previously half-mounted material support area. Therefore screw it for your guidance with two screws in pre-drilled holes directly behind the hole of the front leg of the horse. Then take the try square, which you hold underneath the seat and draw the measurements on the horse. Remove the material support area again, draw the cross lines with the try square onto the seat and saw 1 cm deep into the wood, followed again by chiselling the groove from both sides.

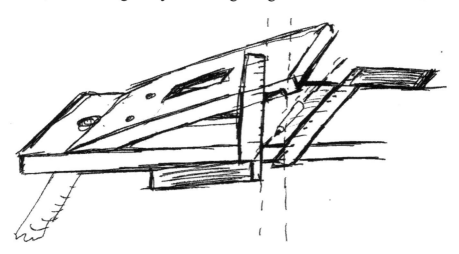

8. Mounting the Material Support Area

Screw the material support area directly behind the front leg like in the first sketch in step 5 with six screws (four in the front, 2 in the vertical board) from above and two additional screws from below through the seat in the vertical board through pre-drilled holes. It makes sense to insert the squared timber, which will be the lever arm, straight away into the notches of horse and material support area as an additional fixation and guide. Maybe you have to widen the groove for the vertical board in the material support area a bit.

9. Preparing the Lever Arm

Saw off a 75 cm long part of the squared timber, this will be your lever arm. It gets several boreholes of different diameters. Drill always on the 8 cm wide side in the middle (4 cm). Drill two boreholes with ½ inch / 1.27 cm from above. The first one is in a distance of 3 cm from the top. Then add 3 cm plus the thickness of your plank (e.g. 5 cm) plus 1 cm and you get the distance for the second borehole (here = 9 cm). Later you fit in between these holes the dumb-head. All further boreholes have a diameter of ¾ inch / 1.9 cm. Three boreholes for the rotation axis of the lever need to be at 20, 25 and 30 cm from the top. Drill the last borehole at 6cm from the bottom. It is for the foot rest.

Drilling the lever arm

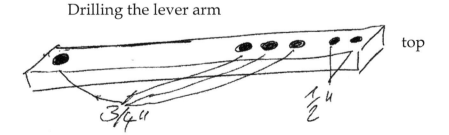

top

$\frac{1}{2}$"

$\frac{3}{4}$"

10. Preparing the Dumbhead

The remaining part of the plank with a length of 25 cm will be your dumb-head. Also here you need to make a hole/slot for the lever, this time 5 cm away from the rear end and exactly 6 x 8 cm in size in the middle of your plank. You have already gained experience with notches. Bevel the upper front edge slightly with a knife and/or a hatchet. So you can use your drawknife from more rearward later on.

An out of centre kerf on the front-side of the dumb-head is well-suitable for a better fixation of small diameter round wood for e.g. shaving the bark off.

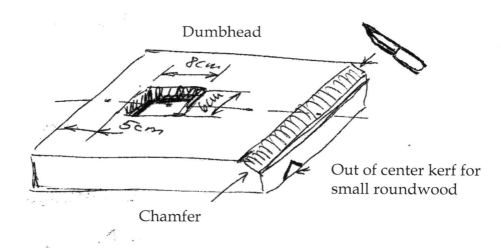

Dumbhead

8cm

6cm

5cm

Out of center kerf for small roundwood

Chamfer

11. Assembling the Shaving Horse

Before you can assemble everything, we also need some carved sticks and dowels. You carve the 30 cm long roundwood with 2 cm diameter in a way that it fits through the ¾ inch / 1.9 cm borehole across through the material support area and so it serves you as axis for the lever arm. With an additional 35 cm long piece you do the same way. This will be your footrest. Now put the lever through the notches of the horse. You lead the rotation axis through the cross-ward boreholes of the material support area and the big topmost hole of the lever. Does the lever swing freely on the bottom side, you don't have to shorten it and you can insert the footrest tightly. Then carve two slightly conical dowels, which measure circa ½ inch / 1.27 cm at their midst. You wedge with them the dumb-head between the topmost small boreholes. You can drive them with a hammer in so that it fits tightly.

12. Improvements on your Shaving Horse

Congratulation for finishing your first difficult project! The dumb-head should bite and now you can work comfortably and seated on your work pieces. But of course there is still room for improvement. For instance there are sharp edges everywhere, which need to be chamfered with a knife so nobody gets injured.

And if you feel like adding a further slot, you can enhance the leverage. Instead of the footrest, made of a carved stick, you prepare a notch 6 x 8 cm, again 5 cm away from the rear in a board which needs to be at least 25 cm long.

Shaving Horse

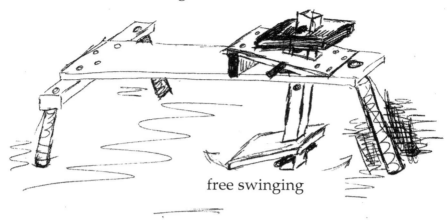

free swinging

You insert this from below onto the lever and push the shortened former footrest as security pin against any slipping down through the bottom borehole of the lever. This results in a longer lever with more pressure and a better posture of the feet during your work.

My shaving horse has a built-in dowel plate at the rear.

Making a Butter Spreader on the Shaving Horse

Such a butter spreader is a fine thing. It is easy to manufacture and it is a good starting project. Besides you can use any cut off wood from other projects. It is similar to a knife. Small children learn with it how to use a knife without using a real one. They are proud to have their own wooden one. In the northern European countries they are common breakfast equipment.

Used Tools

Shaving horse
Hacksaw/Japanese saw
Hatchet or froe, mallet
Drawknife
Carving knife

Material

Piece of greenwood, e.g. birch or alder, 20 cm long, diameter starting at 10 cm

Working Steps

1. Sawing Wood to Length

The piece of greenwood needs to be circa 20 cm long. One centimetre more or less doesn't matter.

2. Splitting Wood

If your piece of greenwood is still a log, split it first into half, then one half into quarters and again halve one of the quarters. This one eight is your starting point for the butter spreader.

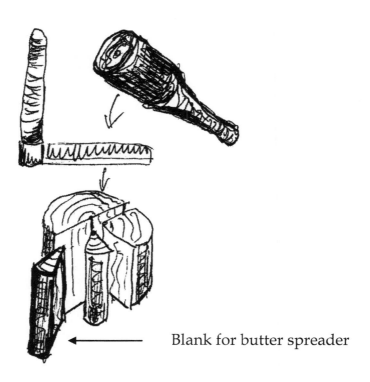

Blank for butter spreader

3. Making a small board on the shave horse

You can pre-process with a hatchet.

Smooth the straightest side of your piece of wood with a drawknife. Turn the blank and create a small board with an even thickness of about 5 mm on the shaving horse.

4. Marking the right shape

Draw with a pencil the shape of your butter spreader on the wood. Work with soft round shapes. These are by far easier to carve than pointed edges. Besides to that, the butter spreader appeals more natural.

5. Carving the butter spreader

First carve the outer shape of the butter spreader with a carving knife. Take care that you always carve "downhill" of the grain. Then chamfer the edges, so that it lies comfortably in the hand. There, where the "blade" is, carve the chamfer a little wider.

6. Final steps

If you carved well, your surface has already become smooth. No surface gets as smooth like one that is made by a sharp blade. After drying you can still rework with sanding paper. Finally, after drying, lay the butter spreader in an oil bath for 24 hours. After taking it out, wipe it properly and let it dry for one or two more hours. Then it is ready for use.

Constructing a Bowl Horse

Now with the shaving horse work will become much easier for you. While you had to invest up to a week of time for the previous project, the bowl horse is relatively fast done. It is used to clamp and hold the wood which is needed to carve a bowl. Actually it is only a log where you take off one half of its 40 cm width. Should you intend to make bigger bowls than 35 cm in length, extend the 40 cm long notch (and so the log) appropriately.

Used Tools

Shaving horse
Hacksaw/Japanese saw
1 ½ inch/3.8 cm auger (brace)
Drawknife, carving knife
Hatchet and/or wide chisel and mallet
Clamps

Material

Straight log, at least 1 m long, 20 to 30 cm diameter
Four pieces of pole wood with 4 cm diameter, length circa 70 cm, for the legs of the bowl horse

Working Steps

1. Sawing in the log

Draw on the horizontally positioned log at the half diameter a horizontal line on both sides. Image your log is 1 m long, I plan to take off about40 cm, where the half is removed. This allows bowls up to 35 cm length. A short section at the end serves additionally as support for making the bowl. And so the important 40 cm are not exactly centred. The beginning of the wood you wish to remove is 20 cm away from one end and 40 cm from the other one. Saw into your log down to the marked centre lines. Make a third cut also 20 cm away from the end and saw up to 1 cm away below the centre lines. On the 40 cm long part you need to remove you make more cuts every 5 to 10 cm. That makes it easier to remove the wood.

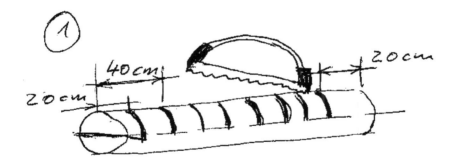

2. Chiselling out the excess wood

With a chisel or a hatchet you remove roughly on a length of 40 cm any excess wood, so that a notch is created. You can smooth it with a drawknife to form a clean horizontal surface. Then put the log upright, so that the below the centre line sawn-in side shows upwards and split the sawn-in half away with the hatchet. Take care that the beginning of the split-off part sits a little above the centre line because the sawn-in end is just 1 cm below. If the horse stands horizontally, this area is slightly bevelled.

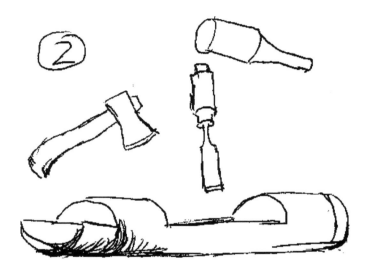

3. Drilling Holes for the Legs

Turn the log around and put it with the cut-out area across the end of your shaving horse. Fix it there with clamps. Take measure from the horizontal bottom and mark two dots both-sided, one 10 cm away from the end on one side and another one 30 cm away from the other end (at the cut in end), so that they are in a 35° to 45° angle from each other. Don't make the angle too small, it needs to stand safely on the ground! There the legs will be inserted. Drill the holes about 8 to 10 cm deep in dependence of the thickness of the log.

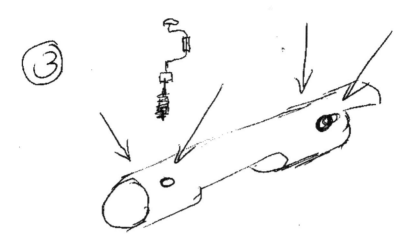

4. Bringing the Legs to Hole Size

Now your shaving horse is really of value, if you are pointing the legs with the drawknife, so that you can drive the legs into the holes. The leg length depends on your height. I prefer a work height of 60 cm. The leg length is here circa 70 cm, including the part which disappears in the borehole. Point the legs with the drawknife at a length of circa 10 cm.

5.

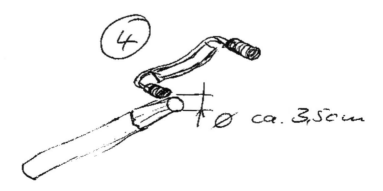

ø ca. 3,5 cm

Assembling

Drive the legs into their holes so that they fit tightly. Then put your horse on a plain, horizontal ground and level it with a spirit level and small chocks. Then take a short piece of batten which needs to be so wide that all four legs of the horse can be marked with it above the chocks while it lies flat on the ground. Draw these lines around the four legs and shorten the legs exactly at these spots. Now nothing should wobble anymore.

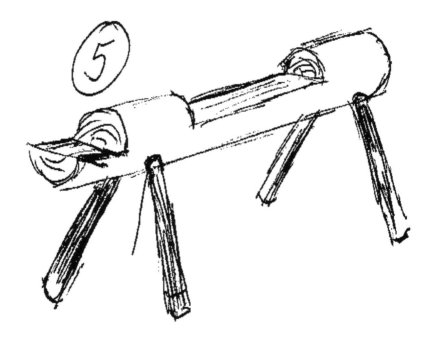

6. Clamping wood in the bowl horse

If you now wish to fix a bowl blank, e.g. a half log, on your horse, you still need a few parallel wood pieces and two wedges. Now lay the half log at one end of the notch, then add the wood pieces as distance holders and drive the wedges from both sides into the other end of the notch. And so the bowl blank sits steady as a rock.

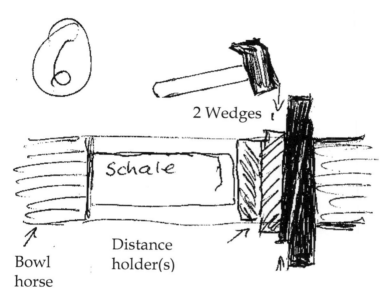

2 Wedges

Schale

Bowl
horse

Distance
holder(s)

And so it should look like if everything is clamped properly. The wedges are hidden by the tools in the picture.

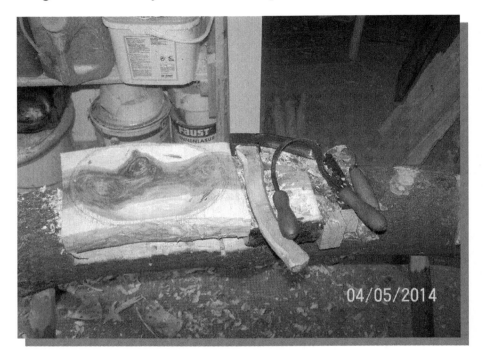

With an adze, a round two-handed scorp (inshave) and spoon knives I hollow out bowls.

Carving a Fruit Bowl on the Bowl Horse

A dough bowl in which the dough for bread is kneaded is known by many. For that a half log is hollowed out beginning from inside. Fruit bowls in the Swedish shape are made by starting to hollow out the bowl from the outside. Such bowls look very stylish on every table with their curved shapes.

Used Tools

Bowl horse with distance holders and clamping wedges
Shaving horse
Bowl adze or bent gouge with a mallet
Drawknife, spoke shave, carving knife, spoon knife

Material

Straight log, circa 35 cm long, 15 to 30 cm diameter

Working Steps

1. Cutting wood to length and splitting it

The log needs to be circa 35 cm long, if the notch of your bowl horse is 40 cm long. One centimetre more or less doesn't matter. When you choose your wood, take care that it grew straight and has nearly no branches. Birch wood is quite suitable for such a bowl. Halve the log with a froe and strip the bark off. Eventually you need to flatten the split side with a side axe.

2. Marking the shape

Clamp the log with wedges and eventually with distance holders on your bowl horse, the flat side shows downwards. If you can draw free-handed very well, it should be easy then to draw the below-shown shape on the log. Do you want to construct the ellipse exactly two nails and a short rope will assist you further. How this is done properly you find on the internet on the below mentioned address[20].

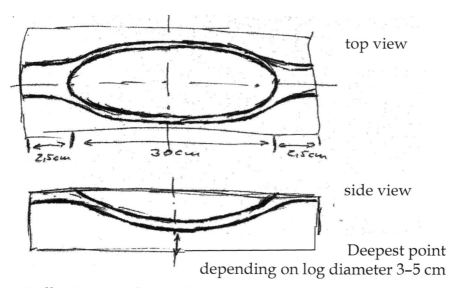

top view

2,5cm   30cm   2,5cm

side view

Deepest point depending on log diameter 3–5 cm

3. Hollowing out the Bowl

Of course hollowing out is the major working step. You do this either with a bowl adze, if such one is among your tools, or with a bent gouge and a mallet. The option with the bent gouge takes usually a little more time. While working with the adze press your upper arm to your side and hit only with the strength of the lower arm starting at your elbow. With this technique your hits are controlled and accurately. Start in the middle of the bowl and work step-by-step towards the side. Then change to the other

---

[20] http://www.franks-fundgrube.de/basteln/kreisoval.html

side of the bowl bench and do the same with the other half of the bowl. Remove the wood layer by layer. Take care at the lower layers and especially at the rim of the marked inner ellipse and take off only small wood chips, so that bottom and rim of the bowl don't get to deep "cuts". Do the fine tuning with a spoon knife and carve a relatively smooth surface of the bowl's hollow. If you own a round drawknife (two-handed scorp, inshave), you can use it as an interim step during your work.

25/05/2013

4. Carving of the outer side

You create the rough outer shape with a hatchet. For that you can work on a chopping block or you use the cut out on the one side of the bowl bench. This has the advantage that there is a contact edge. Begin with drawing a centred ellipse on the bottom of the bowl as well. The bowl will stand later on it. Start with the right or left side of the bowl and chop towards the end. Then start on the other side and finally chop the small radius towards the handle of the bowl. The thickness of the bowl should be even, roughly 1 cm if possible.

5. Smoothing the outer side

For this working step your shave horse comes into play. Here the in the book introduced "dumb-head" shaving horse is more suitable for a bowl than the below shown "bodger" shaving horse, based on a British model. Start with the drawknife and smooth your rough hatchet markings. The fine tuning can be done with the spoke shave to create a fine, clean surface. With a crooked knife you can even undercut the handles of the bowl.

6. Final working steps

Chamfer all sharp edges with the carving knife, so that the user has a pleasant grip feeling. Dry the bowl slowly in a cool, dry room. Oven heat or especially central heating almost always leads to cracks. It takes about one week until humidity deprives from wood. Also important: An even wall thickness avoids cracks too. Should you have used wood like oak, plum or linden, which is prone to drying cracks, put the bowl in a paper bag and fill it with dried wood chips. Have a look after roughly six weeks if the drying succeeded without cracks. If you post process the bowl with sanding paper depends on your personal preferences. Finally I recommend the double coating with linseed oil either with a brush or rubbing it in.

25/05/2013

Work Bench and Pole Lathe

Constructing a portable Work Bench

Since you now have two essential devices to work with greenwood, we slowly dare to get started with more complex projects. A work bench is absolutely necessary for a lot of tasks. An old joiner's bench in the workshop, which you buy inexpensively with luck on Ebay or at a workshop clearance, serves you well. But a simple heavy-weight table with a screwed-onto mechanic's vice does it too. When I was on the road I had often used the seat of my shaving horse until I decided to construct a specialised small work bench with a wooden leg vice (similar to Roubo's work benches) which also fits into my car's trunk. There might be one single component you can't construct yourself: The bench screw or work bench spindle I bought from Dieter Schmidt (Fine Tools shop). My bench screw is a relatively inexpensive Czech made which costs about 45 Euros.

Used Tools

Nearly your complete arsenal plus
Straight chisel 20 - 25 mm wide
Plane
Shaving horse

Material

Dry log of hard wood (beech, sycamore, oak), if possible, log diameter 40 – 50 cm, length 50 – 60 cm
Square timber/bars, circa 10 x 12 cm, ~ 70 cm long
Board, measurements ~ 35 x 6 x 1 cm
Board/plank of hard wood with only a few branches, measurements ~ 90 x 20 x 2 cm
Greenwood: two poles with 7 – 8 cm diameter, 80 cm long for legs and two poles with 4 – 5 cm diameter for stretchers
Bench screw, 5 normal screws, suitable in size

Working Steps

1. Preparing the half log

Strip off the half log's bark properly. Then create an even work area on your half log. Use the side hatchet, drawknife, spoke shave and a plane to achieve this. It is possible to clamp the half log on your bowl bench to fix it. Then draw a line vertically centred with a try square on both end faces and connect both dots on the round side, so you get a centre line.

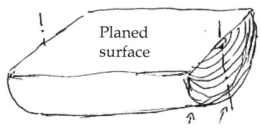

Planed surface

Mark the center line, also from below!

2. Preparing the squared Timber

The upper end of the squared timber needs to get inserted in a notch on the half log and must be flush with the end face. Remove at 10 cm length half of the squared timber. The resulting tenon, 12 cm wide (if the squared timber measures 10 x 12 cm), will then be inserted in the half log. Drill a centred hole 60 cm away from the other end for the bench screw. It should be slightly bigger in diameter than the diameter of the thread. Make a second drill hole 40 cm away from the bottom end with a 32 mm diameter for the stretcher. The notch for the distance board needs to be made 15 cm away from the bottom end for sliding through of the small 6 cm wide board. Drill several 1 cm holes on a length of roughly 6 cm and clean it with a chisel for a 6 x 1 cm large rectangular notch. When testing it the small board needs to fit in without any jiggling but at the same time it should easily slid of the bench screw

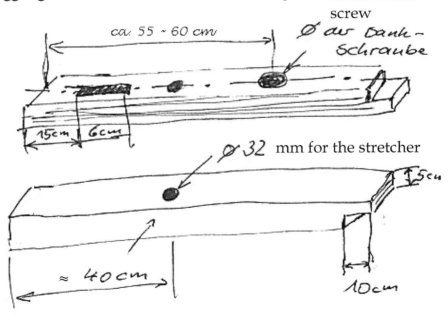

ca. 55 ~ 60 cm
Ø der Bank-Schraube
15cm 6cm
Ø 32 mm for the stretcher
15cu
≈ 40 cm
10cm

3. Carrying out the half Log's Mortise

Choose the half log's end face which was sawn most vertically in relation to the working area. A lighting test with the try square will tell you which one it is. The mortise must be 12 x 5 cm wide, circa 12 cm deep and 5 cm away from the end face and it needs to be parallel to the end face. Even here you drill and do some post processing with the chisel. Flatten the rounding of the half log a little from the mortise to the vertical end face, so that the squared timber can be fitted tightly. You check the tight fit with the tenon of the squared timber. Then drill horizontally from the end face a ½ inch hole through the notch, circa 15 cm deep, without the inserted squared timber's tenon.

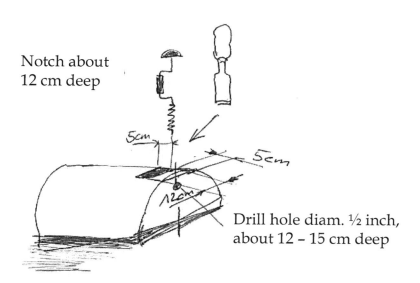

Notch about
12 cm deep

5cm

5cm

12cm

Drill hole diam. ½ inch,
about 12 – 15 cm deep

4. Mounting the squared Timber

Insert the squared timber in the half log's mortise. Put the ½ inch drill in the pre-drilled hole and give a slight hit with a hammer on it. This marks the spot where you have to drill through the squared timber. Do not use this marking but shift the drill 2 mm to the top of the tenon. Insert the squared timber again and drive a slightly tapered 12.5 mm wooden dowel (can be self-made with a dowel maker or carved by you) in. The squared timber is now drawn into the log and fits quite tightly because of the offset of the borehole. Now you can drill holes diagonal from the side at the other end of the half log for the rear legs, diameter 32 or 40 mm. They should be about 10 – 15 cm deep and not go through.

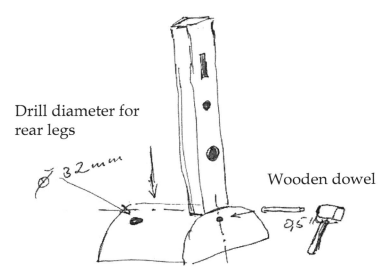

Drill diameter for rear legs

Ø 32mm

Wooden dowel

5. Inserting the Rear Legs

Prepare the rear legs on the shave horse and then drive them into the half log so that they fit tightly. Now you can adjust one for you suitable working height and a horizontal working area by sawing off the rear legs and the squared timber. Be careful, at least 5 cm of wood must be left between the bottom notch of the squared timber and the bottom. And like below it should look by now. In my picture the drill holes and the notch for the squared timber are missing because I made my work bench after the trial-and-error-method.

6. Inserting the Stretchers

At the moment the construction is still a little wobbly on its feet. Stretchers will stabilise it. Make 32 mm diameter pocket holes on the rear legs. Take their height from the squared timber. The rear stretcher is also drilled horizontally centred. Here 1 inch/25 mm diameter is enough. The stretcher's length depends on your needs. Prepare the tenons and two wedges for the longitudinal stretcher, at front of the squared timber 32 mm wide and at the end 25 mm, on the shaving horse. Carve them from dried hard wood. Even at the pocket holes of the rear legs you can add two hidden wedges in case the tenons fit a little loose. Is everything set, your work bench should stand safely and prim. Check once more the horizontal working area with a spirit level and if necessary make corrections on the legs.

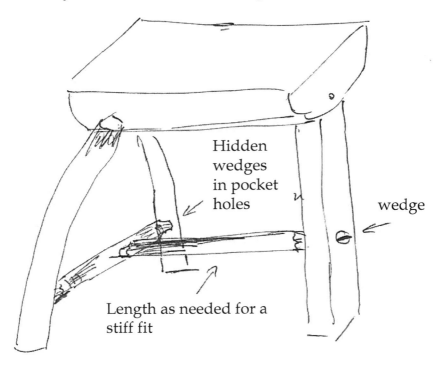

Hidden wedges in pocket holes

wedge

Length as needed for a stiff fit

7. Preparing the small Distance Board

The small board serves as lower counterpart to the lever of the vice and as distance holder. Drill holes and a tenon need to be prepared in reference to the below-shown drawing. For drilling lay the small board on an old one and clamp both of them tightly. So you avoid fraying at the edges of the drill hole on the bottom and you don't have to drill from both sides. The lower board gets mostly destroyed by this procedure.

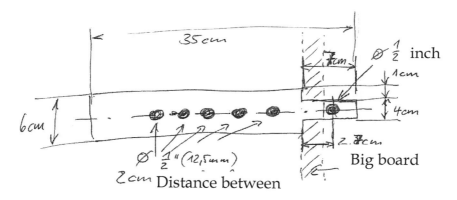

8. Preparing the big Board

Lay a 1 – 2 cm thick board on the ground in front of your squared timber of the work bench as a distance holder to the ground. Now position the big board vertically on it. Fix it centred to the square timber of the front leg and vertically with clamps to the squared timber. You can draw the length of the board by drawing a line on it where the working area meets it. Drill from the back through the already existing hole in the front leg into the board a hole (not completely through!), which is intended for the bench screw and then draw the position of the notch for the small board from behind through the notch of the squared timber on the big board. Remove the big board again, drill like described before the hole for the bench screw completely through and saw the board to length. Chamfer it at a length of 2 cm on its upper edge. make only a small mortise of the size of the tenon, 4 x 1 cm, in the middle of the marked notch for the small distance board. Therefore shorten the marked 6 x 1 cm rectangle for top and bottom by 1 cm, pre-drill and clean it with the chisel. Now everything is prepared for assembly.

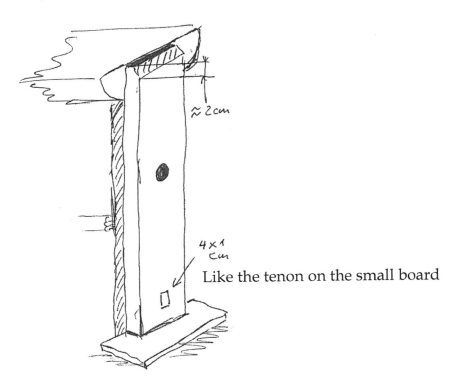

≈ 2 cm

4 x 1 cm

Like the tenon on the small board

9. Mounting the Leg Vice

Set the tenon of the small board into the mortise of the big board and fix it with a wedge or a dowel of suitable size. Remove the counterpart (the "nut") of the bench screw and stick it through the big board. Feed the bench screw and the small distance board through their intended openings of the squared timber of the front leg. Screw the counterpart, the nut, of the bench screw vice versa (normally you countersink it in the squared timber) from behind to the front leg until the big board sits tight on the squared timber. Now fasten the bench screw from the front to the big board with screws and the nut from behind with the squared timber of the front leg. The vice should work by now with an inserted branch as crank. You need a wooden dowel, which you put through the suitable inner hole of the small board, to clamp differently sized work pieces. As you can see in the picture below, the vice is made from two levers with the bench screw as fulcrum. The lower part is the long lever which you can adjust with the distance board and dowel to the right size of the work piece. The short, upper lever will now effectively clamp it to the work bench top.

10. Accessories: Crank and Holes for Holdfasts

I use a debarked branch as a crank. I drilled bigger short pieces of wood with a slightly bigger diameter than the branch ends and screwed them onto the branch to prevent a slipping off. Several holes with 19 mm diameter are drilled into the working area. Two holdfasts can be wedged in them to hold flat work pieces down. My round bench stops which I intended for wedging thicker material didn't prove useful. The bench stops came lose with time and had lots of wobble. Nothing could be wedged tightly.

Result

The small work bench definitely doesn't replace a large work bench like for instance a joiner's bench. But you cannot easily fit a joiner's bench in the trunk of a car, unload it at any place and start working. The small one serves me very well at markets and during presentations or courses. The foundation is a little too light-weight. Therefore I need to put my foot on the stretchers while doing various tasks. But this is rarely disturbing in any way.

Making a Shrink Pot on the Work Bench

Shrink pots are probably a Scandinavian invention. You take a log of greenwood and hollow it out. At the bottom edge you cut a kerf at the inside. Then you insert a tightly fitted, thin and dry wooden board into this notch. The hollowed log dries, shrinks and so the dried board gets caught in the kerf and becomes the bottom of the box. If you then also carve or turn a neat lid you can store in such a shrink pot trivia and jewellery or in the kitchen spices, tea, muesli, caraway or similar things. Naturally shrink pots are not waterproof. But bees wax seals possible cracks. Drinking cold beverages from them would now be possible. Hot fluids would melt the bees wax, smell funny in result and pour out through the little gaps between base and kerf of the shrink pot.

Used Tools

Work bench with vice and jaws for round work pieces
Large auger, e.g. 4 cm diameter hand auger
Straight carving knife, spoon knife
Drawknife, if needed
Maybe a small bent carving gouge in V or U shape fort he kerf

Material

Greenwood: straight, possibly branch-free log, 8 - 15 cm diameter, 12 - 20 cm long (Better start small.)
Thin, split board, 0.3 - 0.5 cm thick as bottom

Working Steps

1. Drilling the starting hole

Clamp the greenwood log with stripped-off bark in the vice of your work bench. For that use one or two jaws like described before. Drill vertically centred and along the pith a big hole through the log, so that a spoon knife fits in and you can start working. Maybe you need to turn the log around and also start drilling from the other side when you feel the auger goes off-centric so that one wall would become too thin.

2. Hollowing out the Pot

Now you roughly hollow out the log with a spoon knife. Work evenly from both sides of the opening. You can check the parallel inner cylinder by looking through the hole. You will see the bulges of wood waiting to be removed. A good way to work is rolling the log on the work bench and hold the knife tightly from the outside in the hollow. This kind of work is gentle to your tendons in your arm. Finally smoothen the inner walls with a straight carving knife so that the get a circa 1 cm even thickness.

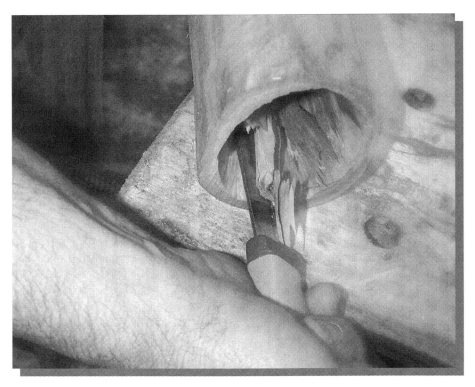

3. Cutting the notch

Draw circa 1 cm away from the bottom of your wooden tube a line at the inside. Set your carving knife as straight as possible and cut vertically into the wood to divide the fibre. In work step two you set the knife angled and cut out the kerf. A small bent V- or U-gouge can be used as well if you own one.

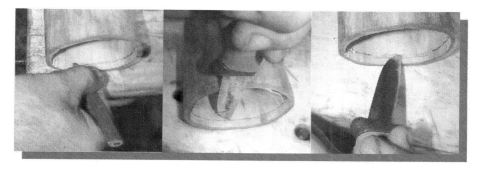

4. Carving the small Bottom Board

Lay a small thin board under the wooden tube and draw from inside the shape of the bottom. Then carefully carve the small board to shape. Chamfer its rim that it fits better in the V-shaped kerf. Test if it fits again and again and adjust with small cuts. By hitting carefully with the knife's handle you insert it, until it sits tightly in the kerf.

5. Drying

Depending on wall thickness, humidity content of the greenwood and room temperature it takes three to seven days for complete drying. You can already see the first success after day one because the small bottom board shouldn't slip out anymore. You should not make a lid before the shrink pot is completely dried, because only then you know the final diameter of it.

Shrink pot with turned lid

Constructing a Pole Lathe – Frame

I would like to introduce my pole lathe model number 6 because it is quite easy to construct, can be used for both, spindle turning and bowl turning, is demountable and therefore easy to transport. All my other models were either not working as expected or only made for one purpose, spindle OR bowl turning. You achieve with a pole lathe, which you use with pure muscle power some talent and a good feeling for rhythm that result in turned wooden products. Place yourself with this machine at a handicrafts market and you will reach a lot of attention and many people will talk shop with you. By now I know some full-time greenwood craftsmen from Great Britain who claim that the rhythm of a pole lathes gives their life a rhythm which also means calmness and strength. In this respect I admit that I can switch off completely and relax while working. Let's get started with constructing the frame.

Used Tools

Shaving horse, drawknife
Normal hacksaw and an electrical fret saw or a chainsaw
Brace with 40 mm and 12.5 mm augers
Straight carving knife

Material

Dry plank from hardwood (the heavier, the better), circa 5 – 10 cm thick, 20 – 25 cm wide and 1.60 – 1.80 m long
4 pieces of pole wood (green), circa 1.50 m long with circa 8 cm diameter as legs

2 pieces of pole wood (green), circa 1.50 long and 5 – 6 cm diameter
2 x 12.5 mm wooden dowel, each 12 cm long

Working Steps

1. Sawing a Long Hole in the Plank

My plank is 1.60 m long, 20 cm wide, 5 cm thick and it is birch wood. Oak, Sycamore or ash wood would be even better suited because they are heavier and more solid. You need to make a 4 cm wide and 1 m long slot in the midst of the plank. The poppets are inserted into it. Draw a centre line, drill at each end of the long hole a 4 cm diameter hole, draw connection lines of the holes with a batten and saw out the long hole with the fret saw. It takes some time with a normal blade. An advantage offers a saw blade which can saw along the fibre. Don't you push too much forward otherwise the saw blade might run away from its vertical direction. Before you start sawing, drill also two vertical holes in 10 cm distance from the two other holes on the centre line, which means at 1.60 m plank length, each 20 cm away from the left and the right end. There the vertical poles for mounting bungees, which will do the retraction, will be inserted.

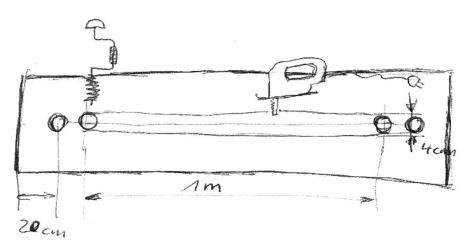

2. Drilling Holes for the Legs

Then drill holes for the legs with 4 cm diameter. The holes are each 8 cm away from the sides. Both holes which point to where you'll be standing when turning, are 12 cm away from the left and the right, the others which point away from you are 8 cm away. Draw additional lines for drilling which go through the drilling centre in a 45° angle towards the long sides of the plank. This line is the direction of your drill showing outward from above. Set the auger in an angle of 65 to 70° to the horizontal line and drill the hole angled to the bottom and outward through the plank.

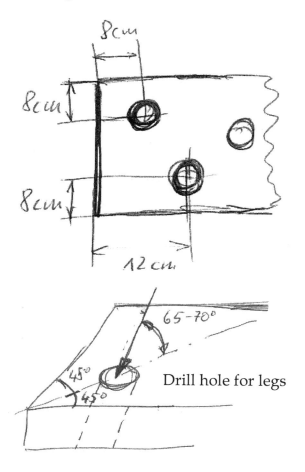

Drill hole for legs

3. Making Legs

Saw four legs at a length of circa 1.40 m. Make a tenon with a drawknife on the shaving horse so that they fit through the angled boreholes for legs and still tower circa 3 cm above the plank. You can saw the exact length for a safe and sound horizontal stand and the right working height at the end. A spirit level assists you to set your plank straight, the height from the bottom should be roughly 1 m for a 1.70 to 1.80 m tall person. Slight wobbles on uneven ground or legs with not exactly 100% in length you adjust by spreading the legs and/or turn one leg slightly. If your legs wobble too much in the holes you can easily fasten them with small wedges hammered in from the top.

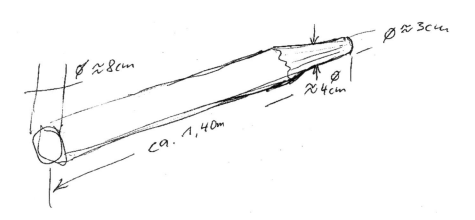

4. Making the Vertical Posts

That you can use bungees for retraction, you still need circa 1.50 m long vertical posts next to the long hole. You need to make a tenon at the lower side with a drawknife on the saving horse so that they stand as vertically as possible in the boreholes. You drill the post on the top end with 12.5 mm diameter, circa 10 cm away from the end. Insert a tightly fitted ready-carved dowel through the borehole, which sticks out 3 cm on both sides. There the bungees are hung up.

Wooden dowel

The current stage without a vertical post looks like this. You'll make the poppets shown on the picture later on.

Constructing a Pole Lathe – Poppets for Spindle Turning

The lathe is designed for bowl turning and spindle turning. I recommend starting with spindle turning because you don't need any special tools. You only need standard woodturning chisels and gouges. In this case a minimum 2.5 cm wide shallow roughing gouge, a 12 mm wide lady finger gouge with a fingernail shaped bevel and an at least 2.5 cm wide straight chisel. With these tools you can do nearly everything. My poppets for spindle turning are kept quite simple. It is easier to make them with squared timber.

Used Tools

Ryoba Japanese saw for cross-ward and long cuts
Rasp for straightening, if needed
Brace with 25 mm and 10 mm augers
Shaving horse and drawknife
2 wrenches - width 17 mm and width 13 or 14 mm depending on your nut size
Bench grinder, metal saw, steel file, 10 and 12 mm drill for steel
Work bench with vice

Material

Dry log or square timber (hardwood) 10 – 15 cm diameter/width + height, 70 cm long
Straight pole wood, diameter 3 – 4 cm, 1.5 m long
Threaded rod M 12 from the DIY-store, 3 nuts M 12
80 cm batten 4 x 3 cm as tool rest
1 – 2 mm thick metal sheet, 15 – 20 mm wide, 12 cm long
1 screw M 10 x 80, 2 nuts M 10
Linseed oil

Working Steps

1. Sawing the Poppets

Cut the log/plank in the middle, so you get two 35 cm long pieces. Decide which ends faces down and saw it in a way that a 4 cm wide tenon with 10 cm length can be plugged through the long hole of the lathe, wobble-free if possible. It should stand quite properly in a 90° angle to the plank. If you work with a chisel instead of the Ryoba, a rasp will assist you to straighten the tenon.

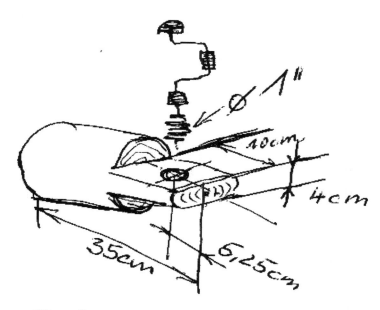

2. Drilling the Tenon

It is necessary to make a 25 mm drilling through the midst of the length axis for wedging. If the tenon sits on the plank in the long hole, the drilling needs to reach under the plank so that the wedging creates tension. Should you use, like me, no accurate measurements, put the poppets in the long hole and draw from below the thickness of the plank on the tenon. The auger diameter needs to reach circa 5 - 8 mm into the plank and so you can mark the the point where to start drilling. In case you stick accurately to my measurements (which isn't a condition), then the drilling is 5.25 cm away from the bottom end of the tenon on the centre line.

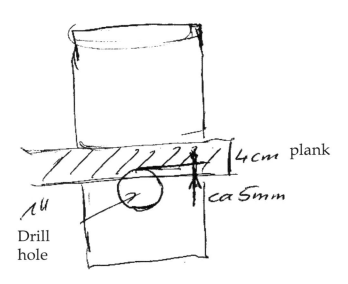

3. Making Wedges

Saw off two 25 cm long pieces of the thin pole wood and shape them as wedges with a drawknife on the shaving horse. Take care that you also decrease the width of the wedge sidewise and so no side pressure is to the hole in the poppet exerted when wedging. That could split the poppets tenon.

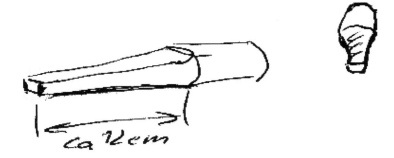

4. Drilling for the Lathe Centres

Our lathe centres, which centre the rotating work piece, need to be inserted centric and parallel to the slot of the lathe-bed. The threaded bar has a metric 12 mm thread, so the core drilling must be circa 10 mm in size. Wedge both poles to the plank, so that they stand exactly side by side and touch each other. The right pole needs to be drilled through completely and the left one needs only a 4 cm deep borehole. The 10 mm auger must be longer than the diameter/the width of one poppet to at least mark the borehole on the other poppet. Does your auger reach 4 cm into the other pole, then you only need one work step. Drill in 20 cm distance from the plank. Consider especially at the beginning of the drilling the direction of the slot in the lathe bed and that you drill horizontally parallel to the plank! You can only correct it in the beginning. Mostly a visual check is enough.

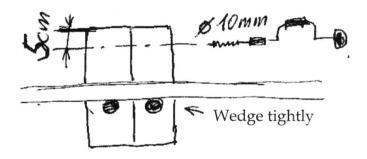

Wedge tightly

Drill direction

from top

5. Preparing and screwing-in of the Centres

Saw from your threaded bar 8 cm and 25 cm long pieces off and grind on one side of each 60° conic tips on a bench grinder. For that hold the thread rod in a 30° angle to the grinding wheel and turn it until a sharp tipped cone is made. Screw with locked nuts the short piece into the left poppet, that only 3 to 4 cm protrude. A single nut wedges it with the poppet. This won't be easy because the thread is not pre-cut. So should you have am M 12 internal thread cutter (die), then pre-cut it as deep as possible. With linseed oil in the borehole it will be a little easier to work. For the crank on the right poppet drill through the metal sheet (Be careful!), 12 mm diameter at the bottom end and 10 mm at the top end. You fix the metal sheet with counternuts at the rear end of the threaded bar. The M 10 x 80 screw, with its head sawn off, serves as crank handle. Especially here file off the sharp burr. For fixation it is locked in the 10 mm borehole of the metal sheet, also with counternuts. The crank handle won't give enough force for screwing the right centre through the poppet. You need to help it by using a wrench, possibly pre-cut the thread in the poppet and also use a lot of linseed oil. In the beginning the thread of the centre works quite stiff but after two to three months it will be much easier to work with.

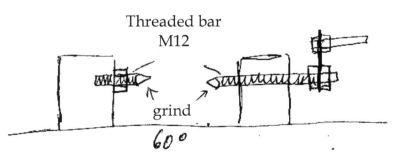

Threaded bar
M12

grind

60°

Screw the centres in with a lot of linseed oil and counter nut.

6. Constructing the Tool Rest

Drill horizontally, centred 4 cm below the centre axis from the front in a right angle towards the centres through the poles with a 25 mm diameter. You also carve 2.5 cm diameter tenons on two 30 cm long pieces of pole wood so that they can be put through the drilled hole and wedged from behind. Then saw out with the Ryoba a 3 cm wide part of the poppet with the tool rest poles inserted as a gauge from above vertically and from the side horizontally. This way the tool rest will get closer to the work piece. Then drill into the tool rest poles every 2 cm 10 mm holes. Two inserted dowels keep the tool rest at the right distance. The batten for it you chamfer on the 3 cm wide side with a drawknife, so that you just leave 1 cm width on top. The intention is that you can change the angle of the turning tool easier while turning.

Side view of a poppet with tool rest:

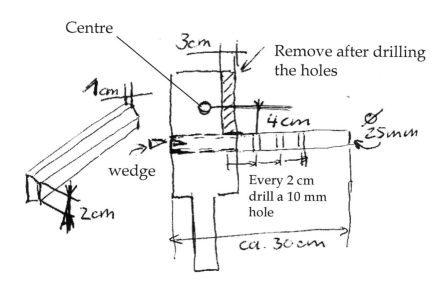

Constructing a Pole Lathe – Poppets for Bowl Turning

Poppets for bowl turning waive threaded rods and create tension by wedging. But the construction on the poppets is not less sophisticated. Therefore two comparative pictures before we start:

It is optimal if the centres for spindle turning „kiss each other". On the left wedge you see the sidewise width reduction well.

Bowl turning poppets: A long and a short poppet with different centres are wedged in long holes to the lathe bed. A swivelling arm serves as tool rest (not in the picture).

The left poppet is by far higher than the right one. Even the centre height above the lathe bed is higher – I prefer to turn bowls at breast height. Because weight matters I have also chosen a bigger poppet diameter. Adapt the height to your personal preferences. In these instructions I explain nearly everything without measurements because you should be experienced enough by now to estimate dimensions yourself. Particularly I refer to the insertion of the tips.

Used Tools

Ryoba Japanese saw for lateral and longitudinal cuts
Rasp for straightening, if needed
Brace with 25 mm, 10 mm and 12 mm augers
Shaving horse and drawknife
Work bench with vice
Bench grinder, saw for steel, mechanics vice
Heavy steel hammer
Angle grinder with a disk for steel, if needed
Grill, charcoal, hair dryer
Wood glue, if needed

Material

Dry log or squared timber (hardwood) 10 – 15 cm diameter/width + height, 1 m long
Straight pole wood, diameter 3 – 4 cm, circa 50 cm long
Round steel or square steel rod, diameter 12 mm, circa 35 cm long
1 m batten 3 x 2 cm as tool rest – can also be made from greenwood on the shaving horse
2 wooden dowels, diameter 12 mm

Working Steps

1. Preparing the Centres

Get your grill ready. Divide the piece of round steel, so that one part is roughly 10 cm and the other one circa 25 cm long. Grind again the conic 60° tip on one side and on each other side grind at 1 – 2 cm length a tapered to square. This side will be hit into the wood. Heat the longer piece of steel in the charcoal until it glows orange, at least it has to be red. A hair dryer serves you well to increase the heat of the grill but don't braise anything. Also at the next work step take care of your protection and that nothing combustible is near your work place. Take the steel with grippers from the grill and mount it in a mechanic vice, so that you can bend it at about half its length with a hammer in a 90° angle. Let it cool down slowly, in water steel would get eventually hardened (you don't know its carbon content) and brittle. We don't want that for centres.

 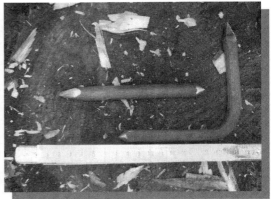

2. Inserting the Angled Centre in the Short Poppet

Prepare the poppets similarly like described in the previous section. Then wedge the short pole to the bed of the lathe. Lay the centre along the slot in the bed on top of the poppet and mark the direction on the poppet. The 60° end of the centre is relevant for the distance of the bore hole from the poppet side. The centre needs to stick out of the poppet side by 2 cm. Drill vertically a 12 mm hole into the pole. Consider the depth of the drilling: The centre must also tower above the pole by 2 cm and for fixation it needs to be driven in 1 – 2 cm deep. For my centre I also added quite a bit of wood glue into the hole for an even safer fit. While you drive in the centre, take care that its direction remains the same. A few hits for correcting the direction are especially successful with a round steel. This also works for adjusting the centre horizontally parallel to the bed of the lathe.

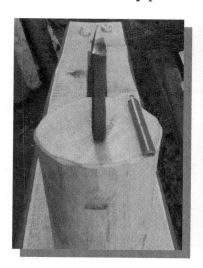

3. Inserting the Centre in the Long Poppet

For marking the drilling on the long poppet you wedge it in the bed, move the short poppet until the centre tip touches it and hit from behind on the centre. Then you drill in this "dent" parallel to the bed and in direction of the slot with 12 mm diameter only so deep that after driving the centre in for 1 – 2 cm the tip protrudes 3 – 4 cm. Use wood glue if needed. A piece of hard wood (e.g. oak) between centre tip and hammer prevents the destruction of the 60° cone. Again – in ideal case the centre tips should "kiss" each other. But 1 – 2 mm discrepancy might not be a problem. Because of rotation between two points the work piece always gets 100 % round. Should you intend to correct it, wedge both poppets tightly and make a few targeted hits with a steel hammer. But do this only after the wood glue is hardened.

4. Swivelling Tool Rest

Drill another 12 mm hole next to the bent centre vertically from above in the poppet and drive in a wooden dowel with wood glue so that it protrudes 5cm. This will be the centre of rotation for the swivelling tool rest. You make again a 25 mm horizontal drilling in the long poppet from the front in a right angle to the centre. If you drill completely through it and wedge it from the back or if you set the tenon of the tool rest support arm in a pocket hole with a hidden wedge doesn't matter at all. The tool rest support arm protrudes the pole by circa 50 cm. You can drill again 10 mm vertical holes every 5 cm through it to get an adjustable stop for the tool rest.

Nearly done!

Only a few things are missing at the lathe. Particularly important is still the treadle whose construction we start in the next section. Your lathe with the inserted poppets for bowl turning looks pretty much like the upper picture. In the bottom picture you see my first attempt of bowl turning on the lathe. I will explain the making of the mandrel, later on.

Constructing a Pole Lathe – the Treadle

You need to drive the machine per foot step with something. A simple board which gets drawn upwards on a fixed rope on one side and lying on the ground on the other side will do. More useful is the construction of a comfortable treadle with a swivelling arm where you don't have to touch your work piece to do the second half while spindle turning.

Used Tools

Work bench with vice
Saw
Hammer
Brace with 10 mm auger
Screwdriver or cordless screwdriver

Material

Boards, 1 m long, at least 12 mm thick (old pallet boards are suitable)
2 battens 3 x 4 cm, 2 m long
2 strong leather strips, 15 – 20 cm long and 3 – 5 cm wide (e.g. an old belt)
60 mm long nails and short screws
1 x M10 x 100 screw with 2 nuts M 10 and 2 washers

Working Steps

1. Constructing the Base Plate

At first measure the trunk of your estate car or van. Its width at the smallest spot is the maximum width of your base plate. 1 m width fits in my car quite well. Therefore my measurements are circa 1.00 m x 0.60 m. You nail on three cross-boards the long boards with two nails for protecting the plate against distorting.

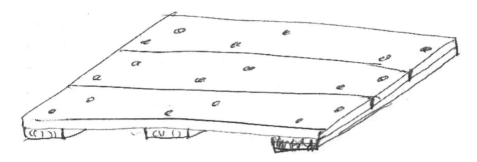

2. Constructing the Swivelling Arm

For the swivelling arm you construct a trapezoidal box from battens and boards with a front opening for the arm. Exactly at that spot is also the drilling for the centre of rotation. As seen from the base plate, the box is circa 30 – 40 cm deep and on the side towards the base plate circa 50 cm wide. Take care that the swivelling arm has enough space to swing to the right and the left at the exit and that you also have 50 cm rotation radius at the front tip. An M 10 screw serves as centre of rotation for the arm. The counter nuts lock it. Don't forget the washers, otherwise the screw will quickly disappear in the wood. The trapezoidal box serves at the same time as foot pedal. Screw leather straps at the bottom towards the base plate from below to the box and fix them on the base plate with five screws on each side. Large headed nails will do as well. Grease the leather well, e.g. with linseed oil, because the hinges need to resist adverse weather conditions. You can cut in a notch in front of the arm through which you can draw the rope.

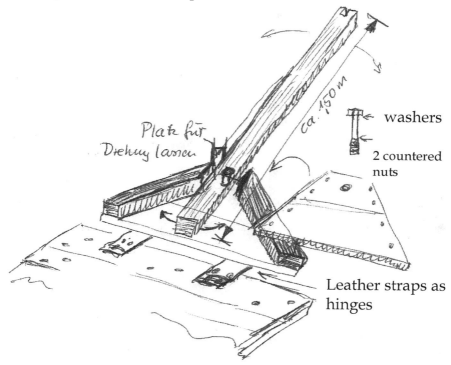

Platte für Drehung lassen

ca. 150 m

washers

2 countered nuts

Leather straps as hinges

Alternative treadle made of a branch fork with a bent branch as swivelling arm

Pole Lathe – Four Kinds of Retraction

So far your pole lathe is ready for use. You only need to think about the retraction of the rope. As rope I use a 3 mm thick tiler's cord of polyacrylic, which you can buy inexpensively as a 50 m coil at a DIY-store. I wind circa 3 m of the cord as coil around the end of the swivelling arm of the treadle and so I have a reserve if I cut the cord accidently with a chisel or if it is worn out badly. Now you need to retract this rope after you have coiled it once or twice around your work piece and you pushed the treadle downwards. That you can release another working stroke it needs to get back up again.

Here several factors can play a role. First there is the strength of your legs which you need to press downwards against the "retraction power" of the treadle. Another aspect is how far on top you step with your foot on the treadle to reduce the used strength (but extend the length of your step). The third factor is the friction of the work piece at the centres. Although linseed oil reduces it, it is noticeable existent. The tighter you fix your work piece between the tips, the stronger the friction. And you should tighten it properly otherwise a strong step on the treadle tears it out away from you. Often there are also visitors in front of you, right in the direction it throws out. You should be careful here.

For you the difficulty is to find a good balance between retraction force, tension of the work piece between the tips and your own leg strength so that you can work persistently and relatively well without getting tired.

Pure Nature: The bent-down Branch

In front of my house stands an old American spruce which was planted by the previous owner in the 80s of the last century. Some videos on Youtube about wood turning on the pole lathe show how a bent-down branch is used as power source. I also wanted to try this myself and I can say, it isn't bad at all to operate the pole lathe this way. I had to try two branches – different in diameter and length. I took off twigs and greenery because they generate too much air resistance like a fan.

Close to Nature: The long Pole in the Ground

My most favourite source for retraction force is a nearly 3 m long and at the bottom end circa 3.5 cm thick hazel rod. You can place it in two branch forks as a tripod and at the end you fix it with a rope and a post in the ground or do it like me and lash it on a tree trunk. For indoor use you can fix it on a ceiling beam, if existent. The pole can be greenwood or even dried wood. Long-fibred wood like ash or hazel, which is also used in bow-making, is suitable. The retraction force of this option is very steady. So I can work in a comfortable rhythm.

This kind of lathe, based loosely on Mike Abbott's Pole Lathe 2000, requires more construction effort.

And so my hazel rod is fixed to the ground. By now I am using pegs.

Physics: Bobbin on coiled-in Rope

I was fascinated by Robin Fawcett's instruction video[21] that I had to test it: A bobbin coiled on four ropes generates retraction. By now this is my first choice when I work outdoors or in a concreted pedestrian zone without any green in sight.

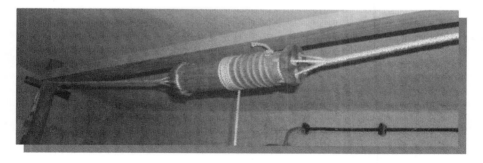

---

[21] https://www.youtube.com/watch?v=jGu_wWZ2iQE

Fast Option: Bungees

If you only want to have little effort than fix the vertical post in the bed of the lathe and span two bungees on top. I prefer 10 mm thick and 1 m long bungees from Obi, a German DIY-store. I use two of them. My vertical posts are circa 1.5 m away from each other. Here the 1 m bungees are fine. Fix the rope down to the treadle on a leather strap. This is wrapped around the bungees for protection against cutting-in and being worn out fast. My bungees wore out quite fast. Careful: Fix the bungees well, because its hooks shouldn't end in your eye in case of slipping off!

Turning a Dibber on the Pole Lathe

A garden dibber requires relatively little work and your skills of a turner don't have to be fully existent yet. However, you'll learn the most important turning techniques with the pole lathe and use all three important gouges and chisels. Working on a pole lathe requires rhythm and coordination of foot, hand and eye. With every downward step you cut into the wood, while drawing back you take the tool one millimetre away from your work piece so it doesn't wear off on the wood and gets blunt to fast. Train this beforehand, best with the roughing gouge. After one to two hours you can do it. Then you can get started.

Actually training is the key to greenwood crafting. Do always the same for a certain amount of time. Someday your hands and your head will remember which way to hold your tools, which work angle the blade has, which leverage effect works best and these movements will become a second nature of you. That is your haptic memory. When I get asked sometimes to demo something I haven't done for quite a while, I sit down for one hour up front and try to recover the skill. My head and my hands start remembering after some time. So it's fine for you to e.g. make four dibbers to train your skills – I am sure you know three more people who have a garden and who you can give one.

Used Tools

Shaving horse
Pole lathe
Chopping block
Hacksaw
Hatchet or froe, mallet
Drawknife
Roughing gouge

Lady finger gouge
Straight turning chisel
Carving knife

Material

Greenwood log, e.g. birch or alder, 25 cm long, diameter at least 20 cm

Working Steps

1. Splitting wood

Quarter the log with a froe.

2. Working with a Hatchet

Remove with a side hatchet as much heartwood of the quarter as you can. If heartwood is used, the work piece will be prone to cracks because the cells of heartwood have taken over a support function for the tree. The sapwood in contrast serves the growth and the transport of water and nutrients. These two kinds of cells have different characteristics while drying – obviously because of their different water content. This results in tension when drying which leads to cracks. Despite that, the colour difference between heartwood and sapwood looks quite nice. Go on with the hatchet and cut off the edges – that means: Shape them as cylindrical as possible. A diameter of 6 – 8 cm needs to remain. Pay attention to straight edges. Per visual checking from one end to the other one you see remaining bulges.

3. Working on the Shaving Horse

Switch to your shaving horse and make your dibber-to-be even more round with the draw knife. Start at one end, take off the edges and hatchet markings and make the piece as cylindrical as possible. Then turn it on the shaving horse and do the other half. Here check once more if your blank is straight. Attention: The wood might splinter if you take off too large chips. Start with small, even chips and work continuously around the wood to get to the shape of your cylinder.

4. Preparing for Turning

Take a gimlet and turn it 2 to 4 times in the middle of both ends and pull it out. In these little dents you'll fit the centres of the lathe. Grease the dents with linseed oil.

5. Clamping between the Tips

Wind the rope once or twice around your work piece, so that while stepping on the treadle the upper edge of your work piece turns towards you. Fit one greased gimlet hole in the fixed centre and turn the crank of the other centre, meeting the other gimlet hole to clamp the work piece. Take care that it is fixed tightly and doesn't wobble. A few steps and turns let the centres work deeper into the wood. Readjust a little with the crank. The work piece must definitely not fly out to the front, shouldn't wobble but retraction of the treadle, e.g. with bungees, needs also to be possible without any big resistance.

6. Using the Roughing Gouge

You make your work piece properly round with the roughing gouge. Vary the work angle, the gouge needs to cut and should not scrape at the surface. When turning electrically the tool scrapes the material off from the wood. In our case, if a man needs to use the few turns with much less rotation speed to take off material, the tool needs to cut. Make grooves next to each other. The roughing gouge is pressed on the tool rest by one hand and the other one leads it at the rear. Take off smaller chips at unbalances of the blank. The rounder the work piece becomes, the easier the turning will be. But don't be afraid, the machine rather stops than that your tool gets torn off from your hand. In addition take care that you don't cut the rope. For the last bit of work push it to the side and move the rotatable treadle too.

7. Smoothing the Surface

Now take a straight chisel to smooth the surface. I use a wide
carpenter's chisel with one bevel in the pictures but the skew
chisel with two bevels works similarly. I personally prefer the
straight one. Hold it at an angle and cut thin wide shavings with
the lower or upper third of the blade by pushing the chisel evenly
to the side (feed). With an angled skew chisel I have made rather
bad experiences because I often hooked into the wood which left
ugly grooves. For professional turners the skew chisel is THE tool
to do nearly everything. It requires a lot of training until you
master it. I remember my great-grandpa using just the skew
chisel to make ladder steps out of squared dry ash on his lathe.

8. Turning the Cone

The dibber needs to be shaped to a cone at a length of 15 cm. To achieve that, use the roughing gouge and the straight chisel. **Turn always "downhill" or horizontal,** so that the tool doesn't push up the fibres "uphill". You start at the end and work layer for layer on increasingly longer ways to the middle. Finish circa 1 cm before the tip of the cone with 0.5 to 1 cm cone tip diameter. From there it should run out cylindrically to the centre. The pointing you will finish with the knife. By the way, the tool rest shouldn't be more than 1.5 cm away from your work piece while turning. So the rear lever arm of the chisel (tool rest to handle) is able to compensate the cutting force on the edge.

9. Turning the Round

The thenar needs to press a garden dibber into the soil at the upper end: This end should be nicely rounded that no edge pinches. You can try to turn the round with the vertically standing edge of the straight chisel. The occurring shavings look like "angel's hair", like Robin Fawcett calls it. For simplicity I use my 12 mm gouge with a fingernail-bevel. The round is created by changing the horizontal work angle for every new step on the tredle. This is an unusual technique to the side for the arm which holds the gouge at the back but this movement is the key.

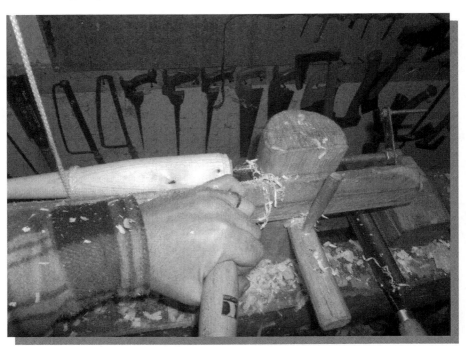

10. Turning Grooves

Draw with a pencil every 2.5 cm starting at the tip of the cone markings on the wood. A step on the treadle with the pencil pressed on the wood draws a line around it. Then set the lower end of the edge of your straight chisel (on skew chisels the tip of the lower end – the heel) at one of these lines. The chisel's edge should be nearly vertical, minimally bent to one side. Then pierce carefully about 1 mm into the wood. Do the same with the other side of the groove, this time bent the chisels edge slightly to the other side to remove the burr. A groove was created which indicates a depth gauge on the dibber. Proceed the same way with all four grooves.

11. Burning the Lines

To make the grooves better visibly, a darker line is burned into the wood. For that we use a hot wire. I e.g. use flower binding wire whose green plastics-isolation disappears quickly while using it. On top and bottom you fix two short twigs as handles. You hold this wire with one hand at the bed of the lathe, lay it in the groove and span it with the other hand. And now you trample on the treadle as much as you can. If aromatic steam of burned wood arises and the groove turns dark brown you have done enough sports. Conclusion: exhausting job.

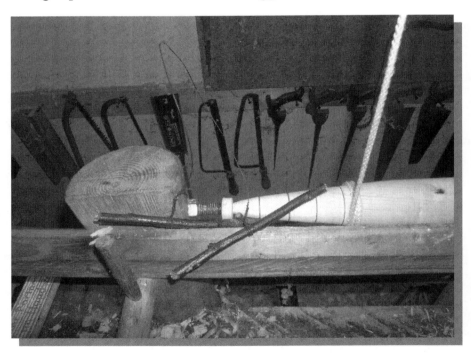

12. Medieval sanding Paper

In greenwood turning sanding paper doesn't work well to make the surface of a work piece easy on your hands. Due to the humidity of wood the gaps between the grinding particles clog up quickly and the grinding effect is gone. I use sanding paper only in rare cases when I work with dried wood on the pole lathe. But the alternative lies in front of you on the ground. Take a handful of just turned wood shavings. Hold it tight on the dibber and turn your treadle a few times. This way you burnish the work piece. Even professional turners use this technique with dry wood. It increases the gloss by pressing the minimally upright-standing wood fibres down.

13. Pointing the Dibber

The last step of manufacturing a dibber is done with a straight carving knife. Take the dibber off from your lathe. At the end there is the cylindrical part which is maybe 1 cm long and 0.5 cm thick which is supposed to be the tip of the cone. Here the centre of your lathe was pressed in. Cut this part off with the knife by sharpening the dibber like a pencil.

Result

Let the dibber slowly dry, then grease it with linseed oil and use it in your garden. While making the dibber you can use all three important turning chisels and gouges for working on the pole lathe and learn their handling. Besides a well useable result of your work it is a good learning process. Therefore use the remaining three other quarters of the original log and keep practicing. Practising wood turning makes you more perfect and you have another three dibbers as a present for others available.

Turning Bowls on the Pole Lathe

The lathe poppets for bowl turning were described in the previous project. Now it is time to start bowl turning. You can't buy the tools for it at the DIY-store. You have to forge the so called "bowl hooks" yourself, ask a blacksmith to make them or order them at an English Blacksmith, e.g. Ben Orford[22] or Rhys M. Harris[23].

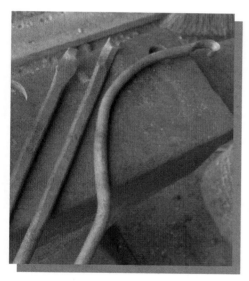

Bowl hooks are available with both-sided or single-sided bevel inside or outside. The bent one serves to turn the nest. Photo: Rhys M. Harris

It is hard to write about the technique of bowl turning without a "living" example. Therefore I refer to five detailed videos[24], which were made by Ben Orford. Study his technique well and listen to his well-explained words. In this book I just write about the preparation of the bowl blank and the mandrel. I explain the mandrel first because it is a prerequisite for the following steps.

---

[22] http://benandloisorford.com
[23] http://www.rhysharris.co.uk/gallery/view_album.php?albumID=11
[24] https://www.youtube.com/watch?v=pNty07IyOAQ&list=PL-NblMYEHHbqyxA8EvbbrYDzHX0aqQmnj

Mandrel for Bowl Turning

Bowl turning with bowl hooks is a small science to itself. I needed all summer long to learn the basics and two more years to master it. An important item for bowl turning is the mandrel.

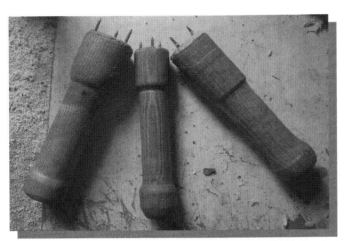

Three mandrels with different diameters for different bowl diameters

Make it exactly like in the previous project per spindle turning on the pole lathe.

Used Tools

All from the previous project
Screwdriver, cordless screwdriver
Angle grinder
Drill bit 1,5 - 2 mm, divider, protractor

Material

Piece of hard greenwood, e.g. beech or ash, 20 cm long, diameter from 20 cm
3 coarse thread screws, 35 – 40 mm long

Working Steps

1. Turning the mandrel

Likewise with the dibber before, use the same procedure to turn the mandrel. The reduction of the diameter on a part of the length leads to better guidance of the towing rope and increases the number of turns per step on the treadle but it is not mandatory. In addition straighten the ends of the mandrel if you didn't saw 100% rectangular. You can do it on the lathe by placing a small lady finger gouge edge upright to the centre of the lathe and turn vertically. Now you have a rectangular area on your mandrel which you can place on the bowl blank. The head diameter depends on the bowl diameter.

For a 15 cm bowl I use a mandrel with circa 6 cm head diameter. For bowls with circa 20 cm diameter I take 8 cm and for smaller bowl with 10 – 12 cm I use a mandrel with 4.5 cm head diameter. Is the diameter of the mandrel too small for the bowl, it loosens quickly and the bowl gets an imbalance and wobbles on the lathe.

2. Holes for Screws

Take a divider. Stick an arm in the centre hole, which was made by the lathe centre, and draw a circle 3 – 5 mm away from the edge of the head. Mark with the protractor, starting from the

circle centre, every 120° three intersections. Drill three holes carefully and take care that the thin drill doesn't break. You can glue in nails, like in the picture, so that they fit tightly in the holes. I personally prefer screws, they hold tighter in the bowl blank.

3. Grinding Screws

Screw the three screws into the holes so that they protrude circa 2 cm. First remove with an angle grinder the heads and then grind them sideward pointed. Take care that the bevel of all three shows in the same direction, so that the mandrel can be hit in grain direction into the bowl blank.

Preparing the Bowl Blank

As promised, here are the instructions how to make a bowl blank. Some colleagues who own machinery use for this a big band saw. I only have a very small one and therefore need to/am allowed to use an axe. During demos this is helpful because I can show the complete bowl making process on-site.

Used Tools

Saw, axe, chopping block, side hatchet, mallet
Divider, pen, protractor with a scale

Material

Piece of greenwood, if possible without branches, e.g. beech or sycamore, diameter at least 15 cm, a little longer than the diameter

Working Steps

1. Splitting Wood

Cleave the log in halves with a froe. Should the surface be quite uneven use the side hatchet to flatten it.

2. Marking

Also, opposite to the split side, flatten the round a bit as parallel to the split as possible. A 5 – 8 cm wide stripe is enough. Mark the centre on the upper side by using diagonals starting at the corners, provided that you cut rectangular in length otherwise measure from the sides. Then take with the try square the distance of the sides and transfer the centre to the bottom side. Draw with dividers the biggest possible circle on the flattened stripe and trace it with a pencil. It serves as orientation for the axe. On the top side draw the biggest possible circle as outer diameter of the bowl and a smaller one which will serve as orientation for centring the mandrel.

3. Working with the Axe

I work from the side toward the centre of the half log. The direction gives me the outer circle on the flat side. In a second step I axe from the other side. I usually work on three levels going from the flat side to the round. At the first level the cut should be vertical to the flat side, the second lever in a 30 – 45° angle to this cut and the third level flattens toward the drawn circle on the flattened round side. The more careful your axe work is, the more easier is the bowl turning later. Other turners use a different technique to rough out the bowl blank.

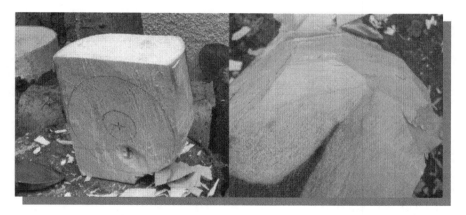

If you're done with one side, do the same to the other part that the blank is reasonable round and symmetric.

4. Inserting the Mandrel

Set the mandrel centrally on the small middle circle of the flat side. Take care that the bevel of the screws goes with the grain. Then hit in the mandrel with a mallet so that the end of the head lies flat on the top side of the bowl. Check for the right angle of the mandrel and adjust with a few taps of the malled if needed. Now the bowl blank is prepared for turning.

Demonstrations and Courses

Let's come to an end with these tools, devices, appliances and machines. Building something by yourself is great but you won't always succeed to 100%. I can help. A few weekends per year I am free, come to you and build with you a shaving horse or a pole lathe and even teach you the basics in using these devices. At craftsmen markets and festivals in towns and villages, at museums and medieval re-enactment events, at fair grounds, at company or any similar events I am also pleased to show you my craft and explain the techniques to guests. The procedure is simple: I cost 250 € a day (8 – 10 hours working time) plus travel expenses and lodging. In summer I am quite modest, a meadow, where I can put up my tent and a shower nearby are enough. In winter a bed inside a house is sufficient. Because the space of my van is limited you need to bring the building material yourself. Currently I can bring the following equipment with me which I permanently extend:

2 pole lathes, one adjustable in height for children
3 shaving horses
Bowl horse
Work bench
Tools for up to five people who work at the same time
Medieval garb (craftsman, circa 13th century)

You'll find material lists for projects in this book. Start generously: It is better you have a little more material than less. For presentations and markets I can bring along a limited amount of greenwood myself.

Demonstrations

Carving spoons and turning wooden bowls, making rustic furniture, crafting twig-pencils with children, making brooms or even demonstrating to visitors how a medieval wood workshop exclusively works with hand tools – I can demonstrate it for you. And this will interest the visitors of your event. I explain a lot and let the guests have a go themselves.

Besides my mother tongue – strictly said, I speak the south-eastern dialect of Meißen which is spoken in the eastern Ore Mountains and around Dresden – I also speak High German and English. I can explain well in both foreign languages, that is what I do. A little Russian, still existing from school days, helps me survive in the eastern European countries.

Demonstration on the pole lathe at a Festival in Zwickau 2013

Courses

My courses are different in length, depending on the topic. I usually teach the basics. To gain mastership you need to invest time and keep practicing. But the why and how of the techniques and work steps I can explain well to you. I organize courses not that often at my small workshop. My space is quite limited and might be rather suitable for individual lessons. In summer I have already organized courses in my garden but even that one is small and there is no flipchart or black board. If you would like to book a course with me, please consider adequate open space. Up to five persons can take part. The courses are suitable for children from 14 years, occasionally even for younger ones.

My topics and duration of the courses:

Cosntruction of a pole lathe and its usage, circa 2 days
Cosntruction of a shaving horse and its usage, circa 2 days
Spoon carving basics (from 13 years), circa 6 hours
Making a rustic stool, 1 day
Broom making (from 12 years), 3 hours

Internet

One of the most important media, which I have been using, is the internet. The most important service for me and my craft is Facebook at the moment. May many complain about it, for organizing international groups with similar interests it is an extraordinary tool. For me it is a source of knowledge, sales market and advertising space at the same time. And so you find my web site there. By entering **www.gruenholzkopf.de** you will reach the Facebook-page of Grünholzwerkstatt Possendorf. Don't be afraid, you do not have to be a member to look at this website. All messages and pictures can be accessed without limits. New photo instructions and daily news are often published there. Members of Facebook also find me under my name **Michael Mirkwied Stibane.** Mirkwied is my name in re-enactment shows.

You even can contact me per e-mail if you have any questions. The address is **mstibs@gmail.com**. I try to respond as fast as possible.

Translations of Tree Names

Latin	English	French	German
Acer	Maple	Érable	Ahorn
Acer campestre	Field Maple	Érable champêtre	Feldahorn
Acer palmatum	Japanese Maple	Érable du Japon	Japanischer Ahorn
Acer platanoides	Norway Maple	Érable Plane, Érable Platane	Spitzahorn
Acer pseudoplatanus	Sycamore	Érable sycomore, Érable faux-Platane	Bergahorn
Acer saccharum	Sugar Maple	Érable à Sucre	Zuckerahorn
Aesculus hippocastanum	Horse Chestnut	Marronnier commun	Gewöhnliche Rosskastanie
Alnus glutinosa	Common Alder, Black Alder	Aulne glutineux, Aulne noir	Schwarz-Erle
Betula pendula	Silver Birch, Warty Birch	Bouleau verruqueux, Bouleau blanc	Silberbirke, Hängebirke, Weißbirke
Betula pubescens	Downy Birch	Bouleau pubescent	Moorbirke, Haarbirke, Besenbirke, ...
Buxus	Common Box	Buis commun,	Buchsbaum

sempervirens		Buis toujours vert	
Carpinus betulus	Hornbeam	Charme commun	Hainbuche, Weißbuche
Carya	hickory	Carya	Hickory
Castanea sativa	Sweet Chestnut	Châtaignier commun	Esskastanie, Edelkastanie
Corylus	Hazel	Noisetier, Coudrier, Avelinier	Hasel
Crataegus	Hawthorn, Thornapple, ...	Aubépine	Weißdorn
Fagus	Beech	Hêtre	Buche
Fagus sylvatica	Copper Beech, Common Beech, European Beech	Hêtre commun, Fayard, pourpre	Rotbuche, Gemeine Buche
Fraxinus	Ash	Frêne	Esche
Fraxinus excelsior	Common Ash	Frêne élevé, Frêne commun	Gemeine Esche
Juglans regia	Common Walnut	Noyer commun	Echte Walnuss
Laburnum	Laburnum, Golden Chain	Cytise	Goldregen
Laburnum anagyroides, Cytisus Laburnum	Common Laburnum, Golden Chain, Golden Rain	Cytise à grappes, Cytise aubour, Cytise faux ébénier	Gemeiner Goldregen
Liquidambar	liquidambar,	Copalme	Amerikanischer

styraciflua	America Sweetgum, sweet gum	d'Amérique	Amberbaum, Seesternbaum
Liriodendron	Tulip Tree, Tulip Poplar	Tulipier	Tulpenbaum
Malus	Apple	Pommier, Pomme	Apfel
Malus sylvestris	Crab Apple	Boquettier, Pommier sauvage	Holzapfel
Morus alba	White Mulberry	Mûrier blanc	Weiße Maulbeere
Morus nigra	Black Mulberry, Blackberry	Mûrier noir	Schwarze Maulbeere
Platanus (Platanus x ...)	Plane, (Sycamore)	Platane	Platane
Platanus x hispanica	London Plane, Lacewood	Platane commun	Ahornblättrige Platane, Gewöhnliche Platane
Platanus occidentalis	American Sycamore	Platane d'Occident	Amerikanische Platane, Westliche Platane
Populus	Poplar	Peuplier	Pappel
Populus alba	White Poplar, Silver Poplar	Peuplier blanc,	Weißpappel, Silberpappel
Populus	Grey Poplar	Peuplier grisard,	Graupappel

canescens		Peuplier blanc de Hollande	
Populus nigra	Black Poplar	Peuplier noir	Schwarzpappel, Saarbaum
Populus nigra 'Italica'	Lombardy-Poplar	Peuplier d'Italie	Pyramidenpapp el
Populus tremula	Aspen Common Aspen, ...	Peuplier tremble, Tremble	Espe, Aspe, Zitterpappel
Prunus	Cherry/Plum	Merisier / Prunier	Kirsche/Pflaume
Prunus avium	Wild Cherry, Sweet Cherry, Gean	Merisier, Cerisier des oiseaux, ...	Vogelkirsche, Süßkirsche
Prunus padus	Bird Cherry, Hackberry, Hagberry	Merisier à grappes, Cerisier à grappes	Gemeine Traubenkirsche
Pyrus	Pear	Poirier, Poire	Birne
Quercus petraea	Ssessile Oak, Irish Oak	Chêne sessile, Chêne rouvre	Traubeneiche
Quercus robur	Common Oak, Pedunculate Oak, English Oak	Chêne commun, Chêne pédonculé, Chêne anglais, ...	Stieleiche
Robinia pseudoacacia	Black Locust, False Acacia	Robinier faux-acacia	Gewöhnliche Robinie

Salix	Willow	Saule	Weide
Salix cenerea	Grey Willow, Common Willow	Saule cendré, Saule gris	Asch-Weide, Grau-Weide
Salix carpea	Goat Willow, Pussy Willow	Saule marsault, Saule des chèvres	Salweide
Sambucus nigra	Elder (not strictly a tree), Elderberry	Grand Sureau, Sureau noir	Schwarzer Holunder
Sorbus aria	Whitebeam	Alisier blanc, Alisier de Bourgogne	Echte Mehlbeere
Sorbus intermedia	Swedish Whitebeam	Alisier de Suède, Alisier de Scandinavie, Alisier intermédiaire	Schwedische Mehlbeere
Sorbus aucuparia	Mountain Ash, Rowan	Sorbier des oiseleurs Sorbier des oiseaux	Eberesche, Vogelbeere
Syringa vulgaris	Lilac, Common Lilac	Lilas commun, Lilas français	Gemeiner Flieder
Tilia	Lime, Linden, Basswood	Tilleul	Linde
Tilia cordata	Small-leaved Lime, Littleleaf Linden	Tilleul à petites feuilles	Winterlinde, Steinlinde

Tilia x europaea, Tilia x intermedia	Common Lime, Common Linden	Tilleul commun	Holländische Linde
Tilia platyphyllos	Large-leaved Lime, Broad-leaved Lime, Largeleaf Linden	Tilleul à grandes feuilles	Sommerlinde
Tilia americana	American Linden, American Basswood	Tilleul d'Amérique	Amerikanische Linde
Ulmus	Elm	Orme	Ulme/Rüster
Ulmus glabra	Wych Elm, Scots Elm	L'Orme blanc, Orme de montagne	Bergulme
Ulmus minor	Field Elm	Orme champêtre	Feldulme, Iper
Ulmus minor "Atinia"	English Elm, Atinian Elm		Englische Ulme
Abies grandis	Grand Fir, White Fir, Balsam Fir, ...	Sapin de Vancouver, Sapin géant	Küstentanne
Abies nobilis, Abies procera	Noble Fir, Red Fir	Sapin noble	Edeltanne
Cedrus	Cedar	Cèdre	Zeder
Juniperus communis	Common Juniper	Genévrier commun, Genièvre	Gemeiner Wacholder

Larix decidua	European Larch, Common Larch	Mélèze d'Europe, Mélèze commun	Europäische Lärche
Larix kaempferi	Japanese Larch, Karamatsu	Mélèze du Japon	Japanische Lärche
Pinus contorta	Lodgepole Pine, Shore Pine, Twisted Pine	Pin tordu	Küstenkiefer
Pinus nigra	Austrian Pine, European Black Pine	Pin noir d'Autriche, Pin noir	Schwarzkiefer, Schwarzföhre
Pinus nigra ssp laricio	Corsican pine	Pin laricio de Corse	Korsika-Kiefer
Pinus sylvestris	Scots Pine	Pin sylvestre	Waldkiefer
Picea sitchensis	Sitka Spruce	Épicéa de Sitka, Épinette de Sitka	Sitka-Fichte
Picea abies	Norway Spruce	Épicéa, Épicéa commun	Gemeine Fichte
Pseudotsuga	Douglas fir	Sapin de Douglas	Douglasie
Taxus baccata	Yew, Common Yew	If, If commun	Europäische Eibe
Thuja plicata	Western Red Cedar, Pacific Red Cedar, Giant Cedar, ...	Cèdre de l'Ouest, Thuya géant, Thuja géant de Californie	Riesen-Lebensbaum

Keyword Register

Bibliography

Abbott, Mike: „Grünholz – Die Kunst mit frischem Holz zu arbeiten", Verlag Th. Schäfer, Hannover, 2000

Edlin, H. L.: "Woodland Crafts in Britain", B. T. Bratsford Ltd., London, 1949

Hill, Jack: „Ländliche Holzarbeiten", Verlag Th. Schäfer, Hannover, 2006

Jaeger, Ellsworth: "Wildwood Wisdom", Shelter Publications Inc, Bolinas, 1992

Lambert, F.: „Tools and Devices for Coppice Crafts", Evans Bros. for the National Federation of Young Farmers' Clubs, 1957

Mills, Edward and Oaks, Rebecca: "Greenwood Crafts – A Comprehensive Guide", The Crowood Press, Ramsbury, 2012

Sundqvist, Jögge: "Schnitzen", Verlag Th. Schäfer, Hannover, 2005

Tabor, Ray: „Grünholz-Vorlagenbuch", Verlag Th. Schäfer, Hannover, 2006

Contact and Imprint

Author and Editor

Michael Stibane
Untere Dorfstraße 7
01728 Bannewitz-Possendorf
Germany

Print and Publishing

Amazon Create Space
http://www.createspace.com

Contact

Telephone: +49 (0) 35206 398790 (ab 17:00 Uhr GMT/UTC+1)
E-Mail: mstibs@gmail.com
Internet: http://www.gruenholzkopf.de
Facebook: Michael Mirkwied Stibane

20259165R00121

Printed in Poland
by Amazon Fulfillment
Poland Sp. z o.o., Wrocław